D1498823

# Innocence Denied

## A Guide to Preventing Sexual Misconduct by Teachers and Coaches

William L. Fibkins

Rowman & Littlefield Education
Lanham, Maryland • Toronto • Oxford
2006

Published in the United States of America
by Rowman & Littlefield Education
A Division of Rowman & Littlefield Publishers, Inc.
A wholly owned subsidiary of The Rowman & Littlefield Publishing Group,
Inc.
4501 Forbes Boulevard, Suite 200, Lanham, Maryland 20706
www.rowmaneducation.com

PO Box 317
Oxford
OX2 9RU, UK

British Library Cataloguing in Publication Information Available

**Library of Congress Cataloging-in-Publication Data**

Fibkins, William L.
  Innocence denied : a guide to preventing sexual misconduct by teachers and
coaches / William L. Fibkins.
    p. cm.
  Includes bibliographical references.
  ISBN 1-57886-313-9 (hardcover : alk. paper) — ISBN 1-57886-314-7
(pbk. : alk. paper)
  1. Child sexual abuse by teachers—Prevention—Handbooks, manuals, etc.
2. Teachers—Professional ethics—Handbooks, manuals, etc. 3. Coaches
(Athletics)—Professional ethics—Handbooks, manuals, etc. I. Title.

  LB2844.1.C54.F53 2006
  364.15'3—dc22

                                                          2005014783

⊗™ The paper used in this publication meets the minimum requirements of
American National Standard for Information Sciences—Permanence of
Paper for Printed Library Materials, ANSI/NISO Z39.48-1992.
Manufactured in the United States of America.

This book is dedicated to Dr. Alan Goldberg and Dr. Richard Pearson, now retired professors in the counseling education program at Syracuse University. Al and Dick were my mentors at Syracuse and taught me the important lesson that professionals involved in close relationships with students need to know how to set clear boundaries, keep their own personal needs in good order, and have a support system available if and when they find themselves becoming too personally involved in a student's life. As this book documents, there are real hazards and risks in guiding and advising needy, vulnerable adolescents. Alan and Dick served their graduate students well by opening up the issue for discussion and offering ways to train and prepare teachers, coaches, counselors, and administrators to avoid taking on friendship, surrogate parent, and savior roles that can lead to sexual misconduct. Needy students are best served by caregivers who are well trained and aware that they, like their needy students, can be at risk, given disruptions, losses, and setbacks in their own personal lives. Best to prepare professionals by raising their awareness rather than making the dangerous assumption that sexual misconduct only happens to professionals in other schools. I believe that awareness can help stem the tide of sexual misconduct and promote open discussions in our schools rather than, as is the case now, seen as a taboo subject and a problem "that can't happen here." I thank Al and Dick for that gift of knowing.

# Contents

*Chapter One*

# Issues in Facing and Solving the Problem of Sexual Misconduct

In this book I argue that there is no epidemic of teacher sexual misconduct in our schools. Nevertheless, too many teachers engage in such misconduct.

As Edward Stancik, the special commissioner of investigation for New York City schools, reports, "I don't want people to think there are massive hordes of child molesters in the schools, but it is certainly true that there are a lot of relationships between adolescents and school staff."[1]

Teacher misconduct is a problem that must be faced and solved. I believe the charge that there is an epidemic of such teacher behaviors is off the mark and, in fact, detrimental to solving the problem. Why? Because the cure put forth is often legalistic, focusing on teachers who are identified as sexual predators as the main culprits, implementing programs to screen and remove predator teachers with past records of misconduct and teacher training that simply gives them guidelines for avoiding sexual misconduct rather than the necessary skills. This legalistic response heightens the anxiety of students, parents, community members, and teachers and may result in a negative school climate where close contact between teachers and students is suspect. Often it gives rise to vigilante groups. Such a climate discourages important and needed personal contact between teachers and students, erodes trust between teachers and students, erodes trust among colleagues in a school setting where everyone is suspect, and erodes trust between teachers and parents who are already struggling to balance the innocence of childhood with a growing national awareness that the world is a dangerous place. This legalistic "cure" can quickly cast a pall over an open and safe school environment when the

1

newspaper headlines and TV talk shows cry that there is an "epidemic of teacher sexual misconduct in America."

I am not suggesting that there are no sexual predators in our schools. Clearly they must be identified early on, screened out, and directed toward help. As I suggest in this book, we need to broaden our training and intervention efforts to educate all teachers about crossing professional boundaries and becoming involved in love and lust relationships with needy students. Long-term, intensive relations between educators and students found in coaching, advising, drama and theater, and club leadership often provide fertile territory for relationships to move into close friendship and even love relations. In chapter 3 I provide an example of the mischief that can occur when I discuss the impact of the early 1970s Title IX legislation that spawned a wave of new sports teams for young women, coached by male faculty members who had no training in how to manage close contact with young women, many of whom saw coaches as adult role models and the key to athletic scholarships and admission to prized colleges and universities.

There are sexual predators in schools, but that is not the whole story of sexual misconduct by teachers. I argue that the majority of teachers who become involved in sexual misconduct are placed in situations with students in which they have no preparation, no training, and no open doors of help that they can enter before it is too late. They are on their own in dangerous territory, as are their needy students. The warning light of danger gets dimmed and there is no flashing light that says, "Stop here for help." The cases I describe in chapters 2–4 include a lot of looking the other way by colleagues, administrators, and parents. They observe teachers engaging in risky behaviors but they, like the at-risk teachers involved, lack the skills for confronting the situation. We need to help teachers become aware of the pitfalls in close contact with needy students and demystify the notions that "it can't happen here" and "it can't happen to me."

Therefore, in this book I argue that the root of the vast majority of incidents involving teacher sexual misconduct lies in the lack of training, supervision, monitoring, and intervention for teachers who have not learned to establish clear professional boundaries and don't see a red light when they become personally involved with needy students in search of a caring adult role model. As educators we need to raise our awareness that it is risky for both students and teachers to expect teachers to help adolescents resolve personal issues without ongoing training, supervision, monitoring, and intervention. As Dr. Ava L. Siegler, director of the Institute for Child, Adolescent, and Family Studies in New York City, suggests, all adolescents are vulnerable. They are looking for someone to emulate and seeking approval. "Yet psychologically they may not be ready to deal with the consequences of physical and emotional intimacy."[2]

Absent these oversight measures, it should come as no surprise to administrators, teachers, parents, and community members that some teachers will be at risk for engaging in sexual misconduct with students. Sexual misconduct can happen in any school given the combination of teachers in need of personal contact, needy students looking for an adult mentor and model, the lack of training for teachers on how to establish and maintain professional boundaries when they become involved in personal contact with students, and the lack of an effective mentoring/supervision process that can identify teachers crossing professional boundaries and intervene before mischief happens. As researcher and psychologist Jan Kinder Mathews suggests, "When you have a needy child and a needy adult, that's just abuse waiting to happen."[3]

I argue in this book that we need to shine new light on sexual misconduct in order to offer the needed protection for both teachers and students. Answering the following questions will better prepare administrators, teachers, union leaders, parents, and community members to mount effective training and intervention efforts:

1. What behaviors represent teacher sexual misconduct?
2. What are the personal and professional conditions that can spawn such behavior? In this book I argue that the majority of cases of sexual misconduct involve consensual relations between needy teachers and vulnerable students and that sexual misconduct is always a possibility in teacher-student relationships that encourage close contact, such as in the role of adviser, coach, and so on.
3. Why have the discussions about teacher sexual misconduct been limited to the legal aspects involved, discussions that focus solely on the teachers involved as sexual predators and ignore the reality that teachers who are otherwise successful in the classroom and respected by students and parents can become involved in sexual misconduct given

a combination of personal and professional troubles in their lives, a need to find a personal connection and relationship, and needy students who are also experiencing personal trouble and seeking a personal connection?

4. Why has framing sexual misconduct primarily as acts carried out by predators and psychotic teachers who need to be weeded out shifted the remedy away from where the real problem lies: providing effective training, supervision, and monitoring for all teachers? We need a broader, more inclusive definition of which teachers are at risk for sexual misconduct.

5. We need to acknowledge that some predator teachers exist in our schools and closely study why they often go undetected. For example, why is it that the climate in some school settings creates conditions in which highly successful, powerful teachers and coaches are able to prey on vulnerable students and ignore boundaries and professional standards without supervision, monitoring, and intervention?

6. Why is it that in many cases of teacher sexual misconduct the victims who come forward are discounted, threatened into silence, and perceived as troublemakers out to ruin the reputation of the school and the teachers involved in the misconduct? Why is it that the institutional reaction is often to destroy the messenger?

7. What are the costs to the teacher and student involved, their families, colleagues, and peers, and the school district?

8. How can training, supervision, monitoring, and quick intervention help teachers understand the hazards and risks involved and avoid misconduct? How can colleagues and administrators intervene when they observe a teacher becoming involved in risky relationships that are evident to all members of the school community except the naive, unaware teacher?

Research concerning physicians who cross professional boundaries and become involved in sexual misconduct sheds light on the problem. Sexual misconduct occurs in every profession that brings caregivers into close contact with needy youth. As seen in the recent revelations concerning Catholic priests, when training, supervision, monitoring, and intervention are absent, there can be tragic consequences for both the professional caregivers and those they are sworn to help. While the identification of sexual predators and the elimination of the practice of administrators' "passing along" such teachers to other school districts is important, ignoring the risk of sexual misconduct for otherwise normal teachers and denying the reality that such behavior can happen to any teacher given the right combination of factors is to leave both teachers and students at risk. I believe looking at the sexual misconduct of physicians offers us an important beginning to understanding how sexual misconduct can emerge in the lives of otherwise healthy caregivers.

In the study "Sexual Boundaries and Physicians: Overview and Educational Approach to the Problem," researcher William Swiggart and colleagues at Vanderbilt University Medical Center suggest that sexual misconduct may include physician–patient sex, whether or not initiated by the patient, and any conduct with a patient that is sexual or may be reasonably interpreted as sexual, including but not limited to sexual intercourse, kissing in a romantic or sexual manner, touching breasts, genitals, or any sexualized body part, inappropriate sexual comments, and initiation of conversations regarding sexual problems, preferences, or fantasies.[4]

Many parents, school board members, administrators, teachers, and community members would no doubt say these kinds of behaviors couldn't possibly go on in our schools. Yet when we look at conditions that spawn such behaviors, the reality is that these kinds of acting-out behaviors can happen to otherwise normal and dedicated teachers. Swiggart is also helpful to our discussion when he cites research by Gabbard (1999) that classifies the majority of physician sexual misconduct cases into the following four psychodynamic categories:

1. The lovesick physician may feel the normal ethical guidelines do not apply in matters of "love." These physicians appear healthy but may be experiencing significant life crises.
2. The limitless physician, with tireless and selfless devotion to patients, may be vulnerable to the demands of difficult patients. This physician avoids conflict and has little ability to limit any patient's request.
3. The predatory physician represents a small but notorious group of physician misconduct cases often associated with severe narcissistic and antisocial personality disorders.
4. The psychotic physician, the smallest group, is mentally ill.[5]

Swiggart adds some other critical considerations to Gabbard's sexual misconduct data when he reports:

1. The family history of physicians involved in sexual misconduct often reflects a lack of clear boundaries. These include an array of childhood trauma experiences from distant and neglectful parenting.
2. Physicians who have difficulty refusing requests for after-hours appointments and meetings are at risk of sexual misconduct.
3. Most physicians who cross sexual boundaries are older and well established in practice.
4. They are naive about the seductive patient.
5. They fail to have clear office policies with the absence of dress codes and excessive familiarity with nurses and staff that impairs the professional atmosphere.

Gabbard and Swiggart's data suggest, as I argue, that, like physicians, most of the teachers involved in sexual misconduct are not predators or psychotics. Yes, predators and psychotic teachers do exist and we must keep these teachers away from students and out of our schools. But the majority of teachers involved in sexual misconduct, like physicians, fall into the category of lovesick teachers who are experiencing a life crisis such as a divorce, death or illness of a spouse, child, or family member, poor health, professional failure, and so on, and seek affection and caring with students, often adoring and needy students. The majority of teachers involved in sexual misconduct are the limitless teachers who become overly involved with students, often seeking out students who are going through some of the same difficult problems these teachers experienced as teens, such as divorce, alcohol, and drug abuse by parents, abandonment, physical abuse, social isolation, lack of friends, poverty, and so on. These savior-teachers think they can save their students from the same pain they felt as children and in the saving process, they take on the role of a surrogate parent, mentor, friend, and sometimes a lover. Some of these teachers were raised by distant and neglectful parents.

The teachers in the case studies I describe in chapter 2 are professionals who have made it, becoming good at what they do and successful in their careers. Without new challenges, professional caregivers like physicians and teachers can become bored and seek excitement in personal relationships. In my observations these can be teachers who are stars looked up to by colleagues, students, and parents. As one teacher told me, "Who would have thought that Dennis, chair of his department, good family life, wonderful kids, would get personally involved with a student? I guess he was just looking for some change, excitement." As Swiggart reminds us, "Physicians are not educated or trained about sexual and/or romantic boundaries." Nor are teachers and other professionals. They are accidents waiting to happen as they try to administer help and support. Without training the red light announcing "danger ahead" doesn't go off for the Dennises of the world. We should not be surprised.

Most of the teachers I describe in chapter 2, like the physicians in Swiggart and Gabbard's research, became involved in misconduct relationships where there was in the beginning a willingness on the part of both the teacher and the student for a caring and loving relationship. Some are searching for the close personal contact that is missing in their personal and professional lives. Others find themselves involved in sexual contact because they are naive about the hazards and risks in close personal contact with needy students and lack the skills to fend off such advances. As reported in the *New York Times*, there were 110 documented cases of sexual misconduct between staff members and students in New York City schools between 1991 and 1995.[6] Most of the cases involved willing participation by smitten students. In many cases the professional involved let his or her own personal needs take over. Or, as in the case of mathematics teacher Joseph C. de Baca (I describe this case in chapter 2), they believe that they are exerting a positive influence on the students whom they are deeply involved with as friends, parent surrogates, saviors, and lovers.[7]

There is a lot of looking the other way in schools, by educators who are untrained to intervene when they see colleagues crossing boundaries. As the research by *Education Week* on sexual misconduct by school employees from March through August 1998 suggests,[8] many educators are wearing blinders, holding on to false assumptions, and resisting the creation of more of an openness/awareness that this kind of activity "can happen here" and the implementation of needed training, supervision, monitoring, and intervention. Here are some of the report's findings:

1. Such behavior happens in all kinds of schools: public and private, religious and secular, rural and urban, rich and poor.

2. Often the setting is in the school building or in cars, motel rooms, or the student's or employee's home.
3. The feeling that sexual misconduct by teachers is not supposed to happen in our district is the dominant theme in school life. As Wayne Huagen, the superintendent of the Hastings, Minnesota, schools, suggests, "In the back of your mind, you know that anything is possible but you don't expect it to occur." A female teacher in Hastings pleaded guilty to sexual misconduct in July 1998, after a four-month sexual relationship with a teenage student. Huagen said, "It's something that always happens in some other part of the country or in some other school district."
4. Often the teachers involved are the most popular and dedicated in the school. In New Tier High School in Winnetka, Illinois, a social studies teacher who was voted the "most liked male teacher" was suspended for fondling a sixteen-year-old girl.
5. Teachers involved as leaders in extracurricular activities such as music, drama, and athletics were more likely to be involved in sexual misconduct with students.
6. Colleagues and administrators are often reluctant to come forward when they suspect something is amiss in teacher–student relationships such as crossing boundaries even when the acting-out behavior is obvious.

Discussing teacher sexual misconduct in general terms without putting a real face on the problem and the personal/professional complications involved in setting safe boundaries can lull us into thinking these kinds of acts are always abnormal and are carried out, as common lore suggests, only by sick people. Addressing these kinds of acting-out behaviors can help us understand where our training, supervision, monitoring, and intervention efforts need to be focused. The following films clearly point out what can happen to teachers as they become involved in or are on the road to sexual misconduct. In these films the profile of professionals at risk for sexual misconduct described by Gabbard and Swiggart clearly emerges. For example, neither of the two teachers has been trained in how to establish clear sexual boundaries. While appearing healthy, they are experiencing significant life crises in their out-of-school relationships, they are tireless and selfless in their devotion to needy students, they are naive about seductive students, they have difficulty in refusing requests for after-hours appointments, and they are older and well established in their teaching roles. No, these films and my overview are not professional case studies. But they help us come in contact with the real feelings, the human needs, the physical attraction, the moral dilemmas that come with the desire to be honorable professionals versus the need to connect with someone on a personal level who offers care, even love, and an escape from the personal and professional troubles of life that we all face. It's a way, albeit a hazardous and risky way, to stop caring for others and be cared for instead.

The film *Carried Away* chronicles the professional and personal dilemmas of Joseph, played by Dennis Hopper, a teacher whose days are spent educating children in a Midwestern farm town.[9] At night he cares for his terminally ill mother. He is in the caring business day and night. He has an on-and-off relationship with Rosalee, a teacher who is struggling to raise her teenage son alone. Despite her numerous declarations of love and her desire to marry him, Rosalee cannot get through to Joseph, who keeps his emotions locked up.

Things change rapidly when Joseph becomes involved with Catherine, a radiant seventeen-year-old student. Joseph discovers his reservoir of feelings for the first time, experiencing a degree of passion and vitality he never thought possible. As film director Bruno Barreto comments, "You have Joseph, a man leading a sedate life in a dead-end relationship with Rosalee, his childhood sweetheart. Suddenly, a gorgeous seventeen-year-old girl, who exudes raw sexuality, becomes his student. They start an affair that turns the whole community upside down, but it awakens within him a passion that ultimately resuscitates his relationship with Rosalee. The film questions all of the concepts of right/wrong in terms of contemporary morality." Joseph is not a sexual deviant out to prey on vulnerable teens. Instead, it appears he in involved in too much caring for others, his students and his dying mother, and is unable to find affection for himself with Rosalee, his longtime sweetheart. He is vulnerable, and when Catherine appears in his class, mischief happens. The pattern that evolves in Joseph and Catherine's relationship is, in my experience, true to life. It begins with untrained teachers who are needy for contact, little or no supervision or monitoring, looking the other way by colleagues and administrators when it is obvious professional boundaries are being crossed; when the affair comes to light it turns the community upside down. Everyone seems surprised and outraged at a drama that was obvious, yet no one acted early on to help Joseph by confronting him and guiding him into needed intervention.

Some of the same conditions, the impact of a life spent caring for others and developing a sense of vulnerability that spills over when an attractive student enters your life can be seen in the film *Mr. Holland's Opus*. Glen Holland (Richard Dreyfuss), a composer and professional musician, takes a teaching job in the newly renamed John F. Kennedy High School. Holland spent several years on the road but now is married.[10] His dream is to spend a few years teaching in order to accumulate enough savings to allow him to return to his true passion in life: composing music. However, events soon change everything. His wife, Iris, becomes pregnant, and in order to provide for her and their new son, Cole, Holland now finds himself having to settle down, buy a house, and teach driver education in summer school to make ends meet. Teaching is no longer just a means to earn money; it has become his family's livelihood.

However, as Ransom Fellowship film reviewer Rick Mattson points out, Holland breaks through to disinterested students by employing radical teaching techniques in the face of conservative opposition, then exercises profound influence on selected underdog students.[11] He convinces his students that playing music is supposed to be fun. His extra work pays dividends in the music program at Kennedy High School, creating a loyal following of students. Although Holland is achieving professional success at Kennedy, he is experiencing growing personal problems at home. His son Cole is found to be deaf and must have special training and schooling. Much of this responsibility is placed on Iris. The fact that Cole cannot hear makes it difficult for father and son to relate to each other. Tensions rise between Glenn and Iris as they try to adjust to the challenges of finding the best care for Cole, Glenn has a greater involvement in school activities such as directing the annual school musical, and Iris spends more and more time alone. The marriage is in trouble. Holland has relationship problems with his wife and is on unsure ground with his son. Glenn is not seeking other female relationships but he is increasingly lonely and emotionally removed from his home. As he grows distant and perfunctory at home, he finds himself at school in stimulating working relationships with talented students, among them Rowena, a beautiful, talented twelfth grade star of the school musical, who mesmerizes him. She has Glenn spinning, quietly demanding he spend more and more time with her and suggesting they move to New York City and start a new life. Although she is just a teenager, she knows what she wants and she wants Glenn Holland.

Unlike Joseph, Glenn Holland knows the hazards and risk involved, but heading off a disastrous relationship isn't easy. Glenn is getting a lot of personal gratification out of mentoring Rowena and it's not just about music. It seems easier for him to be the center of Rowena's interest than deal with the festering problems at home. He doesn't have a trusted colleague or administrator to help him sort out his conflicted feelings. He has to do it on his own and make the difficult choice to say good-bye to Rowena and return home to deal with saving his marriage and finding ways to relate to his son. *Mr. Holland's Opus* vividly portrays how mentors with unresolved personal problems can become involved with needy students. In a real sense Glenn is lucky. He is not naive about the dangers and risks involved for him, his family, and Rowena, and he is able to put on the brakes before mischief happens. But many teachers lack Holland's awareness and ability to confront the situation. As Mattson suggests, those of us involved in teaching know that it a noble but sometimes tragic calling. Teachers cannot completely distance themselves emotionally from pupils' lives. The pressure of teaching can be massive in the workplace and, as we see through Glenn Holland, at home as well.

As I have pointed out, the combination of untrained and needy teachers who are encouraged to become involved in close contact with needy students without adequate supervision and monitoring is risky business. Well-intentioned teachers intent on doing good and caring for students often don't see the hazards and risks involved before it's too late. But there is more to the story. Beginning in the late 1980s there has been a rising drumbeat at the national level to have secondary teachers become mentors, advisers, advocates for students who lack positive adult mentors. They are urged to embrace the concept that their mission needs to be expanded from the role of an academic teacher to include helping students resolve nonacademic problems that may be impacting negatively on their school success and personal well-being. It was at this time that the issue of teachers possibly becoming involved in sexual misconduct with their needy students arose. It became apparent to me in the 1990s, when I was involved in designing programs to train secondary school teachers to serve as advisers and personal adult advocates for students. My work was part of a national effort triggered by the publication in 1989 of *Turning*

*Points: Preparing American Youth for the 21st Century*, which called for teachers to serve as advisers and forge helping and personal relations with students.[12] *Turning Points* recommended that every student be well known by at least one adult in the school. Students should be able to rely on that adult to help them learn from their experiences, comprehend physical changes and changing relationships with family and peers, act on their behalf to marshal every school and community resource needed for the student to succeed. In 2000 a follow-up book, *Turning Points 2000: Educating Adolescents in the 21st Century*, continued to advocate for an important role for teachers as advisers by suggesting that when students make a lasting connection with at least one caring adult, academic and personal outcomes improve.[13] A significant adult who provides support and direction during difficult times can be an important factor in helping students avoid academic failure and a variety of other problems. *Turning Points 2000* concludes that among youth at risk from health or behavioral problems, family dysfunction, poverty, and other stress, the most important school factor for fostering resiliency may be the availability of at least one caring responsible adult who can function as a mentor and role model.

*Turning Points: Preparing American Youth for the 21st Century* and *Turning Points 2000: Educating Adolescents in the 21st Century* highlighted the need for students to connect with caring adult role models to help them navigate through the ups and downs of adolescent life and the important role of teachers in helping students resolve their nonacademic as well as academic problems. The National Association of Secondary School Principals' 1996 report *Breaking Ranks: Changing an American Institution*[14] and the 2004 report *Breaking Ranks II: Strategies for Leading High School Reform*[15] echoed similar recommendations suggesting every high school student have a personal adult advocate to help him or her personalize the educational experience. The *Breaking Ranks II* report suggested that teachers who serve as personal adult advocates will convey a sense of caring so that their students feel that their teacher shares a stake in their learning. The aspirations, strengths, and weaknesses of each student are known by at least one faculty member, and this will aid in engaging students' families as partners in education.

There were other powerful forces at work encouraging teachers to have closer contact with students to help them resolve both academic and nonacademic problems. As the *Public Agenda* report "Kids These Days:

What Americans Really Think about the Next Generation"[16] suggests, Americans think these are uniquely difficult times for kids. More than eight in ten (83 percent) say it's harder to be a kid growing up in America today. For example, Americans are extremely concerned about threats endangering all kids: drugs and crime, sex and violence in the media, and public schools that often fail to deliver education in a safe and orderly way. Yet, as the report suggests, Americans refuse to give up on kids. They care deeply about their well-being and believe that tackling the issue is of paramount importance to society. Most encouraging, they are stubbornly optimistic about the chances of reclaiming the lives of even the most troubled teens. Americans demonstrate surprisingly high levels of caring and sympathy toward young people. In fact, Americans display an extraordinary, almost stubborn, refusal to write young people off as unsalvageable. Almost three quarters (72 percent) say that "given enough love and kindness, just about any kid can be reached." Even the toughest youngsters, teenagers already in deep trouble, can be redeemed given the right amount of effort. And 74 percent say that given help and attention, just about all youngsters can succeed in school. Teachers were looked to as the main players in salvaging troubled students by refusing to give up on them, providing the right effort to help these students reclaim their lives, demonstrating care and sympathy, and giving them help and attention so that they can learn and succeed in school. In a sense teachers were encouraged to take on a quasi-savior role, again without training in the hazards and risks involved and how to communicate on a nonacademic, personal level that has clear boundaries.

The rush to have teachers salvage students from dropping out and facing a diminished future also gained momentum with changing economic, cultural, and social problems happening at the national level. For example, with the increase in family mobility and immigration, it became all too easy for newcomer students to get lost and lose out on a sense of safety, continuity, and belonging when moving into our larger secondary schools. Teachers on the front lines were the best positioned to intervene and guide these students. And the American family was undergoing great changes with the increase in divorce rates and one-parent families, the decline in church enrollment, school PTAs, community groups, and other sources of trust and support, the pressure of time and money including the special pressures on two-career families and lack of opportunity for families to eat and play together, and mounting isolation from positive community influences. We became a nation on the move with less time for child rearing and nurturing. Teachers were pushed into the breach to serve as positive adult models for students who were often home alone, caring for younger siblings, and unsupervised. The role of teacher increasingly included being mentor, adviser, and advocate. But again, teachers were propelled into these roles without training and a clear vision of how to proceed. They knew how to be academic teachers. Students come in, they take their seats, and the teacher teaches, more often than not by lecture. But teachers wondered how they could meet one-on-one with students, encourage them to talk about personal issues, seek help when the student's life story was beyond their helping skills, and be available when needy students need attention. Questions abound. Should I give students my phone number? Should I meet with them outside of school? How do I refer students who are clearly troubled, even suicidal? How do I help a student who is being neglected or abused?

When teachers responded to administrators' requests to have increased personal contact with students, they often said, "I'm not trained for this kind of work." And they were right. The intention to have teachers serve as mentors, advisers, and advocates was admirable but good intentions were not enough. Without training two things seemed clear. First, teachers would fail in their efforts to develop close contact with students. Yes, they might be given the title of "adviser" but over time would lack the skills necessary to be effective in this role, a lose-lose situation for both teacher and student. On a more risky scale, some teachers might become involved in personal contact that was outside professional boundaries, such as meeting a student for dinner, giving gifts and money, visiting students after hours at their home, and so on, placing themselves and their students in harm's way.

Professional conditions that arise from well-intentioned recommendations to alter in a positive way how teachers interact with students can spawn teacher sexual misconduct. The problem is not the worthy and needed recommendations but in the failure to prepare teachers for the tasks and hazards involved. As a result, as I saw in my observations of teachers as mentors, advisers, and personal adult advocates, when it came time to implement the recommendations of the *Turning Points* and *Breaking Ranks* reports—for teachers to become more involved with their students and serve as adult role models in order to overcome the increasing absence of parents from the home due to the changing economic landscape—there was often little direction on how to move from their primary role as academic teachers into a mentoring, advising, advocating role.

In my observations I found two major problems for teachers as they proceeded into this new career alternative, often without training and left on their own. First, as researcher Pedro A. Noguera points out in a study of reform efforts in ten Boston high schools, the schools' attempts to personalize schooling through an advisory system in which teachers served as student counselors during an extended homeroom period held once a week seemed ineffective.[17] Noguera reports, "We sat in on several advisory classes where no advising was occurring. The teachers had no idea how to use the allotted time and most lack experience in counseling." In my experience good ideas, such as having teachers take on advisory roles, quickly flounder without follow-up and training. This is a lose-lose situation for students in need of positive adult connections and for teachers in need of learning how to proceed and be successful as advisers.

Second, the lack of training as advisers can also create problems if teachers do not fully understand their professional boundaries, which opens the door for teachers who are themselves troubled and at risk to sexual misconduct with students. While some teachers, as the Noguera study suggests, resist taking on the role of adviser and continue to maintain their social distance from the personal side of the complex, tangled, and sometimes destructive lives of their students, others will rush into the adviser role and become overly involved with their students. The boundary between helping and becoming a friend, confidante, surrogate parent, even a lover, is hard to see when teachers become overly involved with their students.

Sexual issues and needs dominate teenage life, as do the need to belong, to be accepted, to be cared for, and to be loved. When teenage students find a caring teacher, sometimes they transfer those feelings to that person. Teachers have similar needs for friendship, to be cared for and accepted. And being human, teachers can and will develop problematical personal relations at various stages in their careers and seek out comfort, caring, and support. Many teachers will experience issues related to divorce, death of loved ones, parenting, failure in the classroom, career setbacks, addictions, family dysfunction, issues of poor health and aging, like everyone else. Events in their personal lives can trigger the need for affection, friendship, and close contact with students.

As I suggested in my beginning work on teacher sexual misconduct, a 1996 *Fastback* for Phi Delta Kappa,[18] sometimes the personal needs of students and teachers converge when they are involved in an adviser–advisee helping role that often involves discussions of emotions and where students may share intimate thoughts and feelings that can provide teachers with insights into their problems and motivation for learning. If a teacher's own personal needs for love and affirmation become thwarted, he or she may unwittingly seek to meet these needs through a close involvement with a needy student, a student looking for a caring, loving adult whom he or she sees on a regular basis. This is a potentially explosive situation for both teachers and students headed toward the margins of school life, looking for connection and comfort. In my experience in training teachers, when teachers say, "I am not trained to help students with their personal problems," they are usually on target. Teachers who dive into advising students without training are a threat to themselves and students, as they are at risk of making costly mistakes that can damage their professional and personal lives, the lives of their students and the families they are trying to help, the important work of many well-trained teachers who serve as successful advisers and know their boundaries, and students in need of positive adult contact. The vast majority of at-risk teachers I am talking about in this book are not sexual deviants or teachers who prey on vulnerable students. Rather, they are human and unwittingly find themselves drawn into intimate relations with students that are often observed by colleagues and administrators who more often than not do not use their position as friend and mentor to intervene to help teachers on this self-destructive path.

The major argument in this book is that teachers must be prepared for the role of adviser so they are well aware of the hazards and risks that come with close contact with students. It is better to be prepared than to hide behind the notion found in many communities that this kind of teacher sexual misconduct "can't happen here" or, worse yet, to turn unprepared and untrained teachers loose without a process in place to monitor and supervise teachers and quickly intervene when teachers are seen crossing professional boundaries. Teachers, like students, can become troubled and drift toward the margins of school life.

Given the reality that any teacher, under the right combination of circumstances, can find him- or herself heading toward the margins of school life and at risk to sexual misconduct, how is it that the major focus on the problem has been educating students and parents to report possible sexual offenses, hire more investigators to scrutinize teachers' behavior, conduct criminal background checks, and weed out sexual predators and psychotic teachers? Why is so little emphasis put on training teachers to prepare them for close personal contact and to be aware of the hazards and risks involved? Here is a classic example of how the sexual misconduct issue is being framed by administrators across the country.

David P. Driscoll, commissioner of education in Massachusetts, suggests that schools need to act more vigilantly to protect students from sexual misconduct by educators. Calling for increased scrutiny, Driscoll told *Boston Globe* reporter Anand Vaishnav that school districts have not paid enough attention to the problem.[19] Sexual misconduct is the primary reason that Massachusetts educators lose or surrender their teaching licenses. Even so, the number of teachers disciplined for sexual misconduct accounts for less than 1 percent of the state's 72,000 public school teachers. The commissioner said he wants school districts to work harder to make students feel comfortable enough to report a possible sexual offense by a teacher or another adult in the school. The state defines sexual misconduct as a range of activities that include verbal harassment, improper correspondence with a student, physical abuse, or inappropriate use of threats such as browsing adult websites or chat rooms. In his remarks Driscoll said he plans to urge school boards to consider hiring more staff to investigate cases. He also wants to push for legislation tightening background checks on applicants. Driscoll said he was spurred to do more by recent high-profile cases of alleged abuse by teachers. A middle school teacher in Chelmsford pleaded guilty to raping one of her students, and a high school teacher in Dudley was placed on leave after pleading not guilty to inducing a minor to have sex. In Florida, Massachusetts, a middle school teacher was charged with having sex with a fourteen-year-old boy. Driscoll said, "We're seeing more and more instances, so we have to recognize that they may be there." In the past six years the Department of Education has revoked, suspended, or denied twenty-six teaching certificates because of sexual misconduct. Those cases ranged from suggestive e-mails to a physical relationship.

Unfortunately, nowhere in this reported account is there any mention of training teachers in how to carry on close contact with students while avoiding sexual misconduct. It's all about vigilance, reporting, investigating, and the legal aspects of the issue. There is nothing about how the teachers in Chelmsford, Dudley, and Florida were swept along into such risky and acting-out behaviors. Nor is there any description of the twenty-six teachers who lost their teaching certificates due to sexual misconduct. Some of these teachers may indeed have been predators or psychotics. But we don't know. My guess is that some were naive professionals caught in circumstances they were unprepared to handle.

But what is clear, and Driscoll says it well, is, "We're seeing more and more instances, so we just have to recognize that they may be there." Driscoll is right in suggesting that "they may be there" but he, at least in this interview, places all his bets on vigilance, investigations, and background checks. The result? The plan he promotes still leaves teachers unprepared and without the supervision and monitoring they need. Rather than fostering the notion that any teacher is at risk and opening up the discussion to increase administrator, teacher, parent, and community awareness, he takes the law enforcement, not training, view, which in my experience often forces teachers into not risking close relationships with their students and closing their classroom doors, reducing trust among teachers, reducing trust between students/parents and teachers, labels and isolates teachers who continue to be personally involved with their students, and changes the school environment from a safe and trusting climate into one of increased vigilance and suspicion, an environment that spawns divisions among teachers and leaves them ripe for accusations.

In fact, the events in Massachusetts crystallize the hazards and risks involved when teachers are expected to take on the role of adviser and provide students with a more personalized learning environment without the necessary training. On one hand the dismissal of teachers in the schools of Chelmsford, Dudley, and Florida for sexual misconduct is met with a call for more vigilance, scrutiny and background checks for teachers. Yet at the same time teachers in some Boston high schools are expected to serve as advisers, quasi-counselors for students. Here are two very different approaches. One says to watch closely all teachers' close involvement with students as it can lead to sexual misconduct. The other says we need to have teachers become more personally involved with students and help them resolve personal, family, and health and well-being problems. One approach says to teachers, "Be careful and stay away from close contact." The other says, "Close contact is now part of your role." I believe these two approaches characterize the ways in which schools approach how teachers should interact with students on a personal level. I would suggest that both approaches are flawed as neither includes the need to train, supervise, and monitor teachers or the notion that every teacher, given the right combination of personal and professional circumstances, is at risk for sexual misconduct. It is a subject that is either not talked about or framed only as acts by predators and psychotics.

Again, a look at research by Pedro Noguera helps shed some light on the negative impact of teachers' lack of training in carrying on close relationships with students. Noguera suggests that the efforts in ten Boston high schools to create an advisory system to increase personal schooling and to raise student achievement was ineffective because of a lack of training. The teachers had no idea how to use the time made available through an extended homeroom period held once a week. Most lack experience in counseling. As Noguera suggests, considering the gap between idea and implementation, it is hardly surprising that small learning communities and advisory groups had not improved teacher–student relationships. Boston teachers did not receive even minimal training in how to be advisers, for example, how to carry on helping conversations, guide students to creditable resources in the school and community to deal with personal, family, and health and well-being problems, be advocates for students with fellow teachers and administrators, and, most of all, how to set boundaries with students. Think of the hazards and risks waiting for these teachers and their students in large urban high schools where, as Noguera describes, pervasive student alienation, boredom, strained relationships between adults and students, and a dropout rate often above 50 percent are present. There are adolescents, many needy and troubled and headed for dropping out, seeking advice and a personal connection with advisers who lack training and experience. Maybe sexual misconduct didn't happen in any of the teacher adviser–student contacts, but the opportunities for such boundary crossing were clearly present. The good ideas of the *Turning Point* and *Breaking Ranks* reports resulted in failed efforts because of poor implementation. The Boston teachers, it appears, were sent off on a mission without being well prepared, as perhaps the teachers from Chelmsford, Dudley, and Florida were.

I believe it is time to challenge the argument raised by David Driscoll and other education leaders, that sexual misconduct is largely carried out by predators and psychotic teachers and should be dealt with solely by educating students and parents to report sexual offenses, hiring more investigators to scrutinize teachers' behavior, and conducting criminal background checks. Until now these critics have owned the argument and completely ignored the part that lack of training, adequate supervision, and monitoring play in fostering sexual misconduct among otherwise normal, successful teachers. A draft report by researcher Charol Shakeshaft commissioned for the U.S. Department of Education says, "There are practices that many believe are likely to reduce educator sexual misconduct." Here are some of Shakeshaft's recommendations as described in *Education Week*:

1. Craft written policies that unambiguously describe and prohibit inappropriate educator–student relationships.
2. Screen new and current employees with background checks that include fingerprinting.
3. Centralize record keeping and designate one case coordinator to whom "all rumors, allegations, or complaints are channeled."
4. Make educators, parents, and students aware of the signs of misconduct by educators.
5. Educate employees and students about expectations for behavior, the responsibility to report suspected wrongdoing, and the proper channels for doing so.
6. Change state certification rules to require new educators to "understand the professional expectations and ethics in regard to student relationships."
7. Set up adequate state and federal registries of educators who have engaged in sexual misconduct with students "where future employers or parents can turn to check backgrounds."
8. Revise state policies to protect students of all ages, to require stringent background checks, to mandate reporting to the state of misconduct accusations, and so on.[20]

Not unlike David Driscoll's recommendations, Shakeshaft's focus is on written policies, screening, background checks, investigations, educating students and parents to aware of the "signs" of sexual misconduct, and educating professionals about behavioral expectations. However, Shakeshaft adds another controversial recommendation: implementing a centralized record-keeping system and designating a case coordinator to whom "all rumors, allegations, or complaints are channeled."

Again, what is missing in the report is the need for effective training, supervision, and monitoring of all teachers. Rather, the report emphasizes vigilance, screening, and investigation that, I argue, would establish a climate in which every teacher is suspect and vulnerable to charges that would increasingly flow secretly and unchallenged into a case coordinator's office from any member of the school community who has heard rumors or suspects misconduct. Where are the rights of teachers to defend themselves before a case is secretly built against them? Where is the needed role of the school administrator in being the primary person responsible for supervising teachers? Where is the needed role of teacher union representatives in protecting their members from rumors, possibly false accusations, and complaints? As I have already noted, there is a place for screening and background checks to weed out sexual predators and psychotic teachers. But that effort could create a school climate that focuses on vigilance and suspicion, and welcomes rumor and allegations and labeling that may be false, premature, and in some cases a vendetta against a given teacher. We need to make sure that our remedy to the problem of sexual misconduct doesn't result in a less trusting, safe, supportive, and caring environment for both students and teachers. Some educators took issue with Shakeshaft's finding that more than 4.5 million students endure sexual misconduct in their schools.[21] Shakeshaft says that the best estimate available shows that 10 percent of children face teacher misbehavior, from unprofessional to criminal, between kindergarten and twelfth grade.

Paul Houston, executive director of the American Association of School Administrators, said, "Out of the millions of teachers out there, you're talking about a very small number who are doing inappropriate things. Teachers increasingly fear making even the most innocent gesture, such as hugging a child who is having a bad day." The National Education Association (NEA), the American Federation of Teachers (AFT), and the National School Boards Association (NSBA) all said the report could create a false impression in the public's mind that the physical sexual abuse of students by educators is rampant in schools.[22] The NEA called the report's tone alarmist, and the NSBA suggested that it diminished the problem by appearing to overstate it. Michael Pons, a spokesman for the NEA, said that the 2.7 million member union does not "dismiss the importance of eradicating sexual harassment in the schools" but is concerned about the report's broad focus. "Most people, especially parents, will not read the report and understand some of the nuances of it," he said. "Instead, they will hear that one in ten children is sexually abused in the schools." We need to heed the advice of the NSBA and not diminish the problem by overstating it, alarming educators, parents, and students, and masking the problem as a predator issue.

In reality, the issue includes upping the implementation ante by responding to the need for all teachers to be trained in how to have close contact with students and at the same time avoid the hazards and risks involved. As Paul Houston might say, the key is in knowing when a hug is appropriate to help a child who is having a bad day to refocus on school in a positive way. There is no mystery in making meaningful contact with students. Our words, our body language, our gestures all spell inviting and caring on the one hand or negativity, no entry, on the other. The danger comes when the intent of the contact is unclear.

That's the kind of training I am promoting, training that focuses on developing self awareness among teachers and the sounding an alarm when they cross professional boundaries and become overly involved in their students' personal lives. Training raises the expectation that when a teacher is observed crossing professional boundaries, colleagues will act quickly to intervene and offer guidance and possible referral. Training clearly identifies open doors in the school where teachers involved in possible sexual misconduct can find skilled professionals who can offer advice, counseling, and direction in a safe and trusting atmosphere, professionals who understand the heartaches that can visit teachers, students, and their families when sexual misconduct looms. The model I am proposing moves the dialogue about sexual misconduct from a secretive or "it can't happen here" context into an open discussion that places misconduct where it belongs, as just one of the many problems that can happen to teachers as they move through the highs and lows of their careers. We need to move the discussion of and response to sexual misconduct away from the dark corners of school life where rumors thrive and admit that it can happen in our school and that it's better to have teachers well-prepared rather than deny them the needed skills for close contact with students. We need to normalize the issue of sexual misconduct, not sweep it under the rug or promote the idea that only crazy teachers on the fringe of school life carry out such behaviors.

We need to dispel the notion that there is an epidemic of teacher sexual misconduct in our schools. As clinical psychologist and sexologist Leonore Tiefer asserts, "A new concern for sexual misconduct arose in the 1980s. Although surveys attempted to assess the prevalence of sexual misconduct, they ran into trouble almost immediately. When is a hug sexual? A kiss? Is there a correct way to express caring? What about affection? How can you tabulate these things on a questionnaire?"[23] Edward F. Stancik, special commissioner for investigation in New York City public schools, does not believe the recent rise in reports indicates an epidemic of sexual misconduct in the public schools but that sexual misconduct remains a problem. "We have reached a point where it's almost impossible to deny we have a real problem to deal with," Stancik said. "That's not the same thing as an epidemic or rampant sexual abuse. But it is a problem, one that is not pretty but has to be faced." Stancik suggests that most of the 110 documented cases of sexual misconduct between staff members and students in New York City schools between 1991 and 1995 involved some kind of willing involvement by the smitten students. I would argue that these cases reveal the real problem: untrained teachers in need of a personal relationship connecting with smitten students in need of an adult advocate. Clearly the professional training programs that currently exist and a a professional teaching degree are sometimes insufficient preparation for real-world helping issues.

Researcher Dan H. Wishnietsky is right when he says, "Because of their status and position, educators have a rare opportunity to make a positive impact on the lives of students who may not have a positive role model elsewhere. High school students are impressionable and might possibly encourage improper relationships. At this point teachers must employ special caution by keeping all relationships totally professional."[24] But I argue that simply talking about what teachers should do without arming them with the real-world skills to ready them to "employ special caution," avoid student encouragement of an improper relationship, and "keep all relationships totally professional" will never solve the problem of sexual misconduct in the absence of special training. Just talking about how teachers should behave, giving them written policies and guidelines, and implementing some of Shakeshaft's recommendations, such as a case co-ordinator role in the schools, will have the negative impact of creating a climate for "all rumors, allegations, or complaints" and may actually invite false charges against teachers. This will ruin lives and professional careers and cast a dark cloud of suspicion over all student–teacher relationships. Here are some examples of how the lives of dedicated teachers can be uprooted and sometimes ruined.

After being accused by several students of sexually provocative behavior in a girls' locker room, gym teacher Roland Heller, of Montgomery County, Maryland, saw his career nearly destroyed in early 2000.[25] Suspended from work, he was given fifteen minutes to leave the school, threatened with arrest by the police, and labeled a sexual molester in the public eye. For almost a month Heller's life was a virtual hell. But as time went by police became suspicious about the students' stories. With each retelling the youths embellished their accusations. It was discovered that the gym teacher had disciplined two of the students prior to the alleged incident. Finally a student confessed and the rest conceded the truth: they had made the whole thing up.

Today Heller is back in the classroom but his exoneration has done little to reassure teachers familiar with his ordeal. In the back of their minds they wonder: Could an angry student falsely accuse me of wrongdoing? Would an investigation clear my name or drag it through the mud? As society aggressively tackles the problem of sexual harassment and abuse in the schools, increased awareness of the issue has given some students the idea that an accusation is a powerful weapon for mischief and revenge.

In 1994 Oregon teacher Dan Domenigoni was accused of inappropriately touching several junior high students, who also spread rumors of the charge throughout the school. The story made the television news and for seven weeks Domenigoni was the object of a police investigation. Finally his accusers recanted, admitting they had made up the story in the hope that the teacher would be fired.

James Corleto, a science teacher and girls' track coach at Freeport High School in New York State, presents another example of the damage that can happen to a teacher falsely charged with sexual misconduct. On July 21, 1998, Corleto was arrested on charges that he repeatedly fondled athletes. The *Newsday* headline concerning the arrest was stark: "Track

Coach Faces Molestation Charges: Female Ex-Athletes Report Fondling."[26] The abuse was alleged to have occurred dozens of times from July 1995 to May 1996 in Corleto's van. The students, who were under seventeen, have since graduated and only recently have told their stories, indicating that they "didn't want to talk about it" until now. Corleto was not charged with sexual abuse because the alleged victims could not recall exact dates, but he was charged with two counts of endangering the welfare of a child, a misdemeanor punishable by up to a year in jail on conviction. The police indicated the allegations surfaced in the spring of 1998 when a former student athlete made reference to Corleto while e-mailing a former student over the Internet. Corleto's lawyer suggested, "Imagination was at work. I think this was schoolgirl gossip that got out of control." Corleto had been voted teacher of the year at Freeport in 1997.

Here was a teacher arrested for fondling. Was Corleto's lawyer's assessment on target that "this was schoolgirl gossip that got out of control"? Evidently the jury agreed. It pondered the case for about an hour before reaching its verdict to clear Corleto of the two counts of endangering the welfare of a child.[27]

Yet false charges and labeling are hard to defend against. Our work is to prepare teachers for such a possibility the best we can. Part of our training, supervision, and monitoring to prevent sexual misconduct needs to include making teachers aware of the retaliatory power of students who are heading toward the margins of school life and have strained relationships with adults in their personal and school lives. These students are capable of using aggressive acting-out behavior such as making charges of sexual misconduct. These kinds of charges by marginal students can find fertile ground in a school environment where vigilance, suspicion, rumors, and false labeling of teachers form the chosen model for preventing sexual misconduct.

In the heated everyday exchanges and confrontations between teachers and students, sexual misconduct is only one of the many charges that can be falsely raised against teachers. Any teacher knows that in the open arena of school, one can be falsely labeled as incompetent, lazy, uncaring, unprepared, catering to favorite students, burned out, racist, too old, too young, too inexperienced, too aggressive, unable to discipline, and so on. It goes with the territory. Welcome to the club. Welcome to teaching in a secondary school in America. This territory requires teachers to know their students well and anticipate personal and professional attacks by some students and parents. Teachers, then, need training in how to anticipate aggressive behavior by some students and not be naive, surprised, and unprepared when they are falsely accused and tagged with a number of labels, including sexual misconduct. Students are not unaware of labeling and its powerful impact as they know from firsthand experience and observation of teacher–student relationships that students are often labeled as lazy, unprepared, spoiled, irresponsible, and so on. Charges are easy to mount in secondary schools, both from students and teachers, and thrive in an environment where trust is low and where labeling is allowed to exist without a strong response by administrators and teachers, a response that sends a definite message that this kind of behavior has no place in a trusting school community.

Although researcher Shakeshaft says she has yet to uncover a deliberate case of lying and she's encountered only a handful of cases where an accusation appeared to involve a student's misinterpretation of a teacher's action, Bruce Meredith, general counsel for the Wisconsin Education Association, disputes such contentions. He says he has been involved personally with numerous cases where students later admitted they had lied. Meredith also raises the concern of false accusations that arise from misinterpretation rather than evil intent. For example, a teacher could put a comforting arm around a shoulder and the student could view it as harassment. He indicates, "Those are allegations where there's an enormous degree of unreliability in reporting. At worst, what you might find is some inappropriate decisions being made. The teacher might not be respecting the student's boundaries. But it's not criminal conduct."[28]

There are valuable lessons to be gained from examining the subtle aspects of sexual misconduct involved in the charges against teachers Heller and Domenigoni and the observations of Bruce Meredith. First, we need to acknowledge that both teachers and students are at risk for sexual misconduct. Teachers become at risk by crossing professional boundaries and becoming too involved in their students' personal lives but also by being naive and not prepared for aggressive labeling by students they may have alienated. For students the risk can arise from being drawn into close contact with teachers without being aware of the hazards, risks, and even dangers to themselves, or by students who choose to aggressively respond to a teacher they dislike by making sexual misconduct accusations.

The bottom line is that in the often anonymous world of our large secondary schools, it is wise for both teachers and students to know where they are heading in teacher–student relationships. Not every teacher has the advantage of wisdom and support from caring colleagues who are willing to help and intervene. The same can be said of some students, who may not have parents who care and monitor their activities and peers who are ready to help and intervene. There are needy teachers and students in search of close personal contacts to make up for the loss of care, even love, in their lives. Sometimes, as in the case of teachers Heller and Domenigoni, there may be students whose parents and adult models have pushed them away, not been available to help when trouble came into their lives, some who may be truly abandoned and alone. As any experienced teacher knows, it is not uncommon for alienated students to transfer hostile and negative feelings they have toward parents onto unwitting teachers who don't see the anger and resentment coming. Not every teacher is experienced and savvy about such acting-out students. Our work is to not let them remain naive and unaware of the hazards and risks of close contact. My message to administrators and teacher leaders who are responsible for the professional development and well-being of teachers is: make sure your teachers are prepared to handle the various aspects of sexual misconduct and not become either victims or victimizers.

Unfortunately the discussion of teacher sexual misconduct to date, not unlike the debate going on in the Catholic Church over priest sexual misconduct, has a limited focus on the legal aspects and liabilities involved in sexual misconduct. Much of the focus for school administrators, teachers' union leaders, and education researchers has been on how schools can screen out sexual deviants who prey on vulnerable students, stop the practice of administrators "passing along" a teacher with a past record of sexual misconduct to another district without warning, and limit teacher education to explanations of the legal risks for crossing professional boundaries. I believe this approach is shortsighted in that it targets only teachers who may be sexual deviants as potential victimizers and omits, even denies, my argument that every teacher is capable of sexual misconduct given certain conditions and frames the sexual misconduct issue simply as one of the pathology of the professional involved rather than creating an awareness that lack of training and supervision may also be the culprits.

We need to expand the definition of which teachers are at risk to sexual misconduct beyond sexual deviants and address the notion that every teacher can become at risk to sexual misconduct given a confluence of professional and personal life changes that have negative consequences and that the training of teachers as advisers move beyond simply informing teachers of the legal liabilities, including training teachers to know where and how to draw the line between professional care and unprofessional conduct in close interpersonal relations with students.

Administrators need to do a better job of screening out teachers who have a history of such behavior. But, as I argue in this book, our work to prevent teacher sexual misconduct also needs to focus on how administrators, teacher leaders, and colleagues can intervene to help the majority of teachers who unwittingly find themselves on the verge of or actually drawn into sexual relationships with students because of their own problematic personal lives, lack of training and the failure of members of the school community to intervene when they see a colleague crossing professional boundaries. These teachers are often successful in the classroom, well-liked, and admired by students and parents but fail to see the red light warning that they are becoming too emotionally involved with a student. In my experience, they teach in schools that lack a red light—an alarm system that should go off when sexual misconduct looms. Many of the teachers I identify in this book are successful professionals who at some point in their careers found themselves driven by emotions and off course, headed for trouble but left to solve their own problems.

When administrators and colleagues observe a teacher taking a student to lunch or dinner, writing daily or weekly notes of support, serving as friend and confidant, and giving the student gifts, the potential for sexual misconduct exists. In fact, many teachers involved in such inappropriate behavior do not become sexually involved with their students, but they do become involved in ways that may be seen as "too intimate" by parents, administrators, or colleagues. This kind of inappropriate behavior needs to be addressed early on through training, ongoing supervision, and monitoring by colleagues. Many times such behavior may be simply naive as untrained teachers may be unaware of the potential problems that can arise from such conduct. Without appropriate training and supervision, actual sexual misconduct or the appearance of inappropriate behavior can happen and bring with it trouble and turmoil for the individuals involved—the teacher, his or her family, the student and his or her family. It can also create a lack of trust in teachers in general for students and parents. And it can force teachers into closing their doors and looking the other way when they see students headed toward the margins.

Damage can be done to all concerned regardless of guilt or innocence and create a chilling effect on teacher–student relations in general. The message conveyed to other teachers, sometimes directly stated by administrators, teachers union officials, or colleagues is, "Pull back. Don't become involved." But this message diminishes the ability of teachers to work with students who need close contact that is positive, helping, and affirming. And just as detrimental, sexual misconduct often keeps teachers stuck in the one-dimensional role of being academic teachers only, no longer willing to risk being an adviser or learn effective helping skills and left instead to maintain their social distance from the real needs of students and not able or expected to use their natural helping skills when they see a student headed toward the margins of school life, wrapped in a cocoon with a sign that says, "I don't do help, kid; find someone else." Consequently both teachers and students lose out. The teachers' natural helping skills are held in check and students needing mentors find their teacher's door closed to such help.

Without proper training and intervention techniques, sexual misconduct can occur and radically, instantly alter the school climate in a negative manner. The stakes are high for school districts, too high, that every teacher might possibly become involved in sexual misconduct. But the good news is that school districts can act to ensure that their teachers are prepared for close contact with students so they can avoid sexual misconduct. For school districts to do nothing, to look the other way, or merely inform teachers of the liabilities is to skirt their responsibilities. Like several dioceses within the Catholic Church, they need to do more than take a legalistic approach that merely lists liabilities for professionals who are expected to be involved in helping students who are marginal and need adult attention, support, and modeling. Professionals who work in close contact with needy clients, whether they be physicians, teachers, or clergy, need training to prepare them for this work.

Regarding Catholic priests, about one in ten of the alleged incidents of sexual abuse by priests in the United States over the past half century took place in Catholic schools, with 5.1 percent occurring during school hours.[29]

Among nearly 4,400 Catholic priests and deacons, 4 percent of priests were alleged to have committed such acts. The Catholic Church's omission of turning priests loose without training in how to become involved in intimate helping relations and set boundaries is a classic example of what can happen when ongoing training and supervision are absent. Such omission invites trouble and heartaches for all concerned and diminishes the important helping role that professionals can offer in times of need. In a real sense, teacher sexual misconduct has many parallels with the Catholic priest scandal, where trust has been diminished, every priest is seen as a potential victimizer, and the important helping role of priests to those in need is clouded in suspicion and their gift of helping others in need is put on hold or approached with caution. But the most glaring parallel is the lack of training and supervision for teachers, priests, and other professionals to ready them for the hazards and risks inherent in delivering care and support to others in a period of great change and uncertainty.

Here is an example of the problem of relying solely on the legalistic approach of using background checks. The diocese of Rockville Centre, Long Island, New York, began conducting background screening of clergy and other church personnel in the spring of 2004.[30] So far the diocese has completed a total of 22,571 background screenings of the priests, deacons, religious, lay staff, and volunteers who serve in diocesan agencies or any of the 134 parishes in the diocese. According to Sheehan, the background screening is part of the diocese's larger effort, which includes training teachers, staff, and volunteers how to be on the alert for cases of sexual abuse and how to report it. Ellen Puglisi, director of the Diocesan Office for the Protection of Children and Young People, said, "The program helps make people aware of the warning signs that a child is being abused or a person is looking to abuse a child." But here again we find no evidence that there is an effort to train priests, religious educators, and teachers on how to establish boundaries when they are involved in close contact with teens, nor any systematic effort to develop a supervision, monitoring, and intervention plan to head off sexual misconduct. The emphasis is on screening out predators who are sexual abusers rather than training each person who is involved in offering care to troubled teens on how to avoid sexual misconduct. That includes priests, teachers, and religious educators who are not, as Puglisi suggests, "looking to abuse a child," but are caregivers who find themselves involved in a close relationship that, as researcher Jane Kinder Matthews describes, involves a needy child and a needy adult. Troubled teens often turn to their church when they need help with personal issues such as divorce, a failed personal relationship, family illness or death, school and peer problems, or addictions. If they come in contact with untrained caregivers, mischief and harm can happen. Dr. Sylvester P. Theisen, professor emeritus of sociology at Saint John's College in Collegeville, Minnesota, reminds us that professional training programs for priests and religious educators remain as they always have been—negligent.[31]

I hope this book will bring school leaders like David Driscoll onboard and help them view the solution to teacher sexual misconduct as lying in effective training, supervision, and monitoring. Keep the legal means necessary to weed out the small number of sexual predators and psychotics but begin to emphasize training, monitoring, and supervision as the cornerstones of an effective education and intervention plan.

In closing this chapter, I want to acknowledge the contributions of researcher Charol Shakeshaft and education leaders such as David Driscoll in helping raise the awareness of educators and civic leaders about the issue of sexual misconduct. While I take a different approach on how to best solve the problem of sexual misconduct, I believe their contributions have sparked a needed national debate.

Chapter 2 will focus on case studies of teachers who become involved in consensual relationships with needy students and how these cases might have been prevented. What is startling about these cases is how easy it was for teachers to drift into these relationships, lacking any training, supervision, or intervention. They were accidents waiting to happen.

Chapter 3 will focus on the risks involved in long-term, intensive, and intimate relations between educators and students, such as the kind that can be found in male faculty members coaching female athletes. This is fertile territory, I believe, for relationships to move into close friendship and even love relations. In this chapter I provide a classic example of the mischief that can happen when I discuss the impact of the early 1970s Title IX. It was a risky environment for sure but, school leaders and parents never saw the risks involved for teachers and students until the cases of sexual misconduct began to emerge, often with the victims being vilified and accused of a vendetta against successful, well-liked, and politically connected coaches who were community icons.

Chapter 4 will focus on cases of predator teachers and how these cases might also have been prevented. Again in these cases, what is startling is the lack of training, supervision, monitoring and intervention when these educators were clearly trying to lure and pressure vulnerable students into sexual activities.

Chapter 5 will present a training program administrators can implement to prepare teachers and coaches on how they can avoid sexual misconduct by creating clear boundaries with students. The chapter will also focus on how educators can pass on this training to teach students how they can establish clear boundaries in relationships with peers, teachers, coaches, and adult mentors.

The cases in each chapter clearly point out the need to provide adequate training for all teachers and the need to supervise and monitor teacher behavior and act quickly when behavior that is out of the norm appears.

## NOTES

1. Edward Wyatt, "Schools Show Jump in Reports of Sex Abuse," *New York Times*, 23 May 2001, 1, 7 (B).

2. Margot Slade, "Yes, Statutory Rape Is Still a Rather Big Deal," *New York Times*, 11 June 1995, 9 (E).

3. Caroline Hendrie, "Abuse by Women Raises Its Own Set of Problems," *Education Week*, 2 December 1998, http://www.edweek.org/ew/vol-18/14women .h18 (accessed 13 August 2004).

4. William Swiggart, Karen Starr, Reid Finlayson, and Anderson Spickard, "Sexual Boundaries and Physicians: Overview and Education Approach to the Problem," Vanderbilt University Center for Professional Health, 2001, http://mc.vanderbilt .edu/root/vumc.php?site=cph&doc=742 (accessed 13 August 2004).

5. G. O. Gabbard, J. D. Bloom, C. C. Nadelson, and M. T. Norman, eds., *Psychodynamic Approaches to Physician Sexual Misconduct* (Washington, DC: American Psychiatric Press, 1999), 205–23.

6. Bob Herbert, "An Ugly School Situation," *New York Times*, 17 May 1995, 19 (A).

7. Caroline Hendrie, "Experts Convene on Sexual Abuse by Teachers," *Education Week*, 9 April 2003, http://www.edweek.com/ew/ewstory.cfm?slug= 30abuse.h22 (accessed 8 August 2004).

8. Caroline Hendrie, "Sex with Students: When Employees Cross the Line," *Education Week*, 2 December 1998, http://www.edweek.org/ew/vol-18/14abuse .18 (accessed 13 August 2004).

9. Fine Line Features Synopsis, *Carried Away*, http://www.finelinefeatures .com/carried/synopsis.htm (accessed 2 September 2004).

10. ChucksConnection Film Review, "Mr. Holland's Opus," http://www .chucksconnection.com/holland.html (accessed 2 September 2004).

11. Rick Mattson, "Mr. Holland's Opus," http://ransomfellowship.org/ M_MrHolland.html (accessed 2 September 2004).

12. Carnegie Council on Adolescent Development: Task Force on Education of Young Adolescents, *Turning Points: Preparing American Youth for the 21st Century* (Washington, DC: Carnegie Council on Adolescent Development, 1989), 1–10.

13. Anthony W. Jackson and Gayle A. Davis, *Turning Points 2000: Educating Adolescents in the 21st Century* (New York: Teachers College Press, 2000), 140–44.

14. National Association of Secondary School Principals (NASSP), *Breaking Ranks: Changing an American Institution* (Reston, VA: National Association of Secondary School Principals, 1996), 1–20.

15. National Association of Secondary School Principals (NASSP), *Executive Summary of Breaking Ranks II: Strategies for Leading High School Reform* (Reston, VA: National Association of Secondary School Principals, 2004), 1–6.

16. Steve Farkas and Jean Johnson, "Kids These Days: What Americans Really Think about the Next Generation," *Public Agenda* (1999), 8–9, 11, 13, 16–19, 25–26.

17. Pedro A. Noguera, "Special Topics: Transforming High Schools," *Education Leadership*, May 2004, http://www.ascd.org/publications/ed_lead/200405/ noguera.html (accessed 4 June 2004).

18. William L. Fibkins, *Preventing Teacher Sexual Misconduct* (Bloomington, IN: Phi Delta Kappa Education Foundation, 1996), 8–9.

19. Anand Vaishnav, "Top Official Targets Abuse by Educators: Driscoll to Urge Vigilance," boston.com, 24 August 2004, http://www.boston.com/news/local/ articles/2004/08/24/top_official_targets_abuse_by_ed (accessed 25 August 2004).

20. Caroline Hendrie, "Preventing Sexual Misconduct," *Education Week*, 10 March 2004, http://www.edweek.org/ew/ewstirt.cfm?slug=26abuse-B1.h23&key words=sexual1%20ab (accessed 18 September 2004).

21. Ben Feller, "Sexual Misconduct in Schools Tabulated," Associated Press, 1 July 2004, http://info/mgnetwork.com/printthispage.cgi?url=http%3A// 222.tampatrib.com/news/M (accessed 14 August 2004).

22. Caroline Hendrie, "Report Examining Sexual Misconduct Taps Some Nerves," *Education Week*, 14 July 2004, http://www.edweek.org/ew/ew_print story.cfm>slug+42Abuse.h23 (accessed 22 July 2004).

23. Leonore Tieffer, "On the Therapist's Couch," *Newsday*, 5 January 1997, 37 (C).

24. Dan H. Wishnietsky, "Reported and Underreported Teacher-Student Sexual Harassment," *Journal of Education Research*, vol. 3 (1991): 164–69.

25. Del Stover, "What Happens When a Teacher Accused of Harassment Is Innocent?" National School Boards Association, 16 May 2000, http://nsba.org/site/print.asp?TRACKID=&VID=58&ACTION=PRINT&CID=332& (accessed 9 September 2004).

26. Blanca Monica Quintanilla, "Track Coach Faces Molestation Charges," *Newsday*, 22 July 1998, 29 (A).

27. Tom Demoretcky, "Teacher Cleared of Fondling," *Newsday*, 26 January 2000, 29 (A).

28. Del Stover, "What Happens When a Teacher Accused of Harassment Is Innocent?"

29. Mary Ann Zehr, "Report Tallies Alleged Sexual Abuse by Priests," *Education Week*, 10 March 2004, http://www.edweek.org/ew/ew_printstory.dfm?slug=26Catholic.h23 (accessed 13 August 2004).

30. Peter Sheehan, "Safety for All Is Goal of Background Screening, Training," *Long Island Catholic*, 20 October 2004, 1, 3.

31. Sylvester P. Theisen, "Interfaith Sexual Trauma Institute (ISTI) Book Review of John C. Gonsiorek, ed., *Breach of Trust: Sexual Exploration by Health Care Professionals and Clergy*," 22 April 1996, http://www.csbsju.edu/isti/Book%20Reviews/gonsiorek.html (accessed 13 August 2004).

## Chapter Two

# Cases of Teachers Who Become Involved in Consensual Relationships

What are the costs to teachers and students involved in sexual misconduct, their families, colleagues and administrators, parents, and the school district? In this chapter I focus on teacher case studies that illustrate the personal and professional costs involved and the inability of the school community to intervene when teachers are clearly moving into such risky behavior. I also use data from these case studies to develop a profile of the kinds of teachers and students who may be at risk.

One of the most compelling aspects of these case studies is the need both teachers and students have for an arena of comfort that is often missing in their personal lives. As researchers Robert G. Simmons and Dale A. Blyth suggest, if the individual is comfortable in some environments, life arenas, and role relationships, the discomfort in another arena can be tolerated.[1] Students are less able to cope if at one and the same time they are uncomfortable with their changing bodies, changes in their family constellation, their home, a family move, moving to a larger school, their peers, opposite-sex relationships, or disrupted peer networks and changes in peer expectations and peer evaluation criteria. There needs to be some arena of life or some set of role relationships with which the student can feel relaxed and comfortable, to which he or she can withdraw and be reinvigorated.

As these case studies suggest, students looking for an arena of comfort because of negative changes in their family life, home situation, peer relationships, and so on, often look to teachers for such comfort. However, as I have suggested, in searching for such an arena of comfort, students sometimes connect with teachers who are untrained in close and personal contact with needy students and are themselves troubled by similar issues in their own lives, for example, deteriorating personal relationships, divorce, caring for ill family members, loneliness and isolation, disinterest and bore-dom with teaching, aging, and so on. These teachers may be looking for an arena of life or a set of role relationships with which they can feel relaxed and comfortable, to which they can withdraw and become reinvigorated, as is clearly demonstrated in the character of Joseph in the film *Carried Away*. This pairing of needy students with untrained and needy teachers can be a toxic mix, a relationship that begins with good intentions and barrels into dangerous territory, a relationship that is observed by colleagues who choose to look the other way, gossip about the relationship, or lack the skills on how to intervene and confront and help the teacher and student.

In a sense colleagues are also victims. They see the risky behaviors un-folding but do not act. Looking the other way becomes a pattern in a school community that is supposed to be building trust and caring. In the end, as these cases portray, everyone loses: the teacher and student, their families, colleagues, students who lose trust in teachers, parents, commu-nity members, and so on. Many of these cases could have been prevented with training, supervision, monitoring, and early intervention. The pain that resulted for all involved in this cases didn't have to happen.

The majority of the cases of teacher sexual misconduct involve a con-sensual relationship between needy teachers and students that emerge out of close contact, often for a prolonged period of time. However, a small number of teachers are predators and use their position of authority to lure vulnerable students into unwanted sexual relationships. Therefore our training, supervision, monitoring, and intervention efforts need to head off (1) the kinds of budding consensual relationships I describe in this chap-ter and (2) the would-be predators I describe in chapter 4. The good news is that we have developed a beginning profile of educators who have the potential to be at risk to sexual misconduct. The data from these profiles should help us take the necessary next steps in developing training, su-pervision, monitoring, and intervention programs. Here is an example of such a profile focusing on teachers who become involved in consensual relationships that lead to sexual misconduct:

1. The majority of teachers involved in sexual misconduct do not go into the profession to prey on students or become involved in inappropriate behavior. They are not predators or psychotics.

2. Sometimes teachers involved in sexual misconduct are star teachers and coaches. These are professionals who are involved in close contact with students through extracurricular activities and sports. Some are icons whose success as teachers and coaches has earned them a position of power in the school and community, a position that they feel allows them to ignore boundaries, rules, and regulations and become involved in risky behaviors without being detected.

3. Teachers involved in sexual misconduct tend to justify their behavior by believing that they want their victims to have a deep personal relationship, and sometimes sex, with someone who cares about them.

4. Apparently teachers involved in sexual misconduct easily avoid detection by colleagues and administrators who in fact may be aware of their transgressions but fail to take the necessary steps to intervene to stop the misconduct. As Lora, a female teacher involved in sexual misconduct in my first case, suggests, "People don't want to see it. The education system doesn't want to talk about this. They want to cover it up."

5. Many teachers involved in sexual misconduct don't stand out from the crowd and, as Lora suggests, are normal people who lead normal lives.

6. Often the teacher involved wishes someone had warned him or her early on about the "slippery slope" that can lead to sex with students and that colleagues had warned and confronted them rather than looking the other way or accepting hard-to-believe explanations.

7. Colleagues and administrators need to intervene and help when they see teachers like Lora crossing boundaries.

8. Many of the teachers involved and their families experience great shame, guilt, and regret.

9. There is little sympathy among colleagues for the pain suffered by teachers who cross boundaries, or their families.

10. There is little awareness that crossing boundaries can happen to any teacher given a combination of personal and professional setbacks. Rather, the teachers are seen as black sheep, out of step, and not representative of the vast majority of trustworthy teachers.

# THE CASES OF JOSEPH C. DEBACA AND LORA

This case study puts many of the issues involved in sexual misconduct in perspective and provides us with a beginning road map of how training, supervision, and monitoring can provide early intervention to prevent such behavior. Memories haunt DeBaca[2] as he looks back on his six-year "affair" with a former student that started when she was fourteen: the fear that the police would show up in his classroom to arrest him, the arresting officers who were waiting for him when he returned from a Hawaiian honeymoon, and the visits in jail from his six-year-old daughter. Also gnawing at him is the thought that all of the anguish could have been avoided if someone had warned him early on about what he terms the "slippery slope" that can lead to sex with students. "What would have really helped me is if someone like myself would have spoken to me when I was a student teacher," said the thirty-seven-year-old former mathematics teacher.

DeBaca and another former Las Vegas teacher convicted of having sex with a student discussed their cases publicly in March 2003 at what was billed as the nation's first conference focused solely on the issue of sexual abuse by school employees. DeBaca and another convicted teacher who appeared at the conference said they had convinced themselves that they were exerting a positive influence in the lives of students with whom they were having sex. "I really wanted her to be with someone who cared about her. That's how I justified it." He said he had no intention of molesting students when he entered teaching.

Both teachers said it was not hard for them to hide what they were doing. "People don't want to see it," said the other former teacher, Lora, a thirty-five-year-old mother. "The education system doesn't want to talk about this. They want to cover it up." Lora said teachers who molest students often don't stand out from the crowd. "If it could happen to someone like me, it could happen to anyone," she said. "We are normal people and we have normal lives." Warnings from colleagues might have helped her avoid crossing the boundaries into sex with a seventeen-year-old girl she coached in softball at a high school during her first year of teaching. She added, "Teachers have to start opening their eyes and helping each other."

DeBaca, who served a year in prison, said he wanted to speak to future educators to offer his experiences as a cautionary tale. He suggested that educators should become more skeptical of their colleagues. "There were a few educators who said, 'This looks really inappropriate that you're driving her home and spending time with her.' My explanation was her parents wanted me to keep an eye on her," he recalled. "Most teachers said, 'Oh, it's okay if the parents know.' The atmosphere is such that it doesn't stick out when you see a teacher outside the classroom with a student," he added. DeBaca and Lora say they both suffered great shame and guilt, feelings their families have shared. Both explained that teaching was all they had ever wanted to do and that being barred from the profession was painful for them. However, the participants at the conference, mostly professionals on the front lines of responding to such misconduct, had little sympathy for the pain that the former teachers had caused themselves and their families. The remarks by DeBaca and Lora prompted an angry response from Shannon Knight, a twenty-seven-year-old mother of three from Pahrump, Nevada. "You guys have no right to classify yourselves as a victim," she said, before getting up and leaving the room in tears.

But the heartaches experienced by the students, teachers, and families involved in these episodes can have a positive message for us if we listen to the words of DeBaca and Lora and use their observations to build an effective sexual misconduct intervention. Their words provide us with keen insight into the thinking of teachers heading toward sexual misconduct and the problems that can occur without the necessary training in setting boundaries. I believe their observations can also help us build a beginning profile of teachers who are at risk and move our discussion beyond limiting sexual misconduct to predators and psychotics. Many school districts are already moving in the direction of screening and background checks but unfortunately that's where they stop. What is missing in our school districts is the necessary training, supervision, monitoring, and quick intervention for the entire teaching staff. Now it is time to focus on otherwise normal teachers who, if we borrow from the Swiggart research on physician misconduct,[3] represent most of the professionals involved in sexual misconduct. As softball coach Lora suggests, she was a normal person leading a normal life. But she was also a new and inexperienced teacher, untrained, seemingly unsupervised, unaware of the hazards and risks involved for both her and the seventeen-year-old student involved. DeBaca and Lora ignored the hazards and risks of crossing boundaries, but I believe they are to be commended for their desire to speak to educators and offer their experiences as a cautionary tale.

## THE CASE OF GWENDOLYN HAMPTON

Increasingly, reports of sexual misconduct in the schools involve women educators. Of the nearly 250 cases of alleged staff on student sexual misconduct reviewed by *Education Week*, forty-three of them, or nearly one in five, involved female employees. In five of those cases the victims were girls.[4] The rest were boys in middle or high school, ranging in age from eleven to seventeen. Given such a female-dominated profession as education, such numbers evoke little surprise. However, we need to keep in mind that the possibility of teachers becoming involved in sexual misconduct is still repressed in many communities and the thought of women teachers involved in such behavior is denied. Many school professionals and members of the public believe that most educators would never even consider sexual involvement with a student, and no female teachers would do so.

On the contrary, I suggest that there are teachers who do think about possible sexual involvement with a student, and some of these teachers are women. To think otherwise is to deny such contact can exist and in the end leave teachers without necessary training, monitoring, supervision, and intervention. Therefore, in our work to rid the schools of teacher sexual misconduct, we need to raise the awareness that there are women educators who are at risk to sexual misconduct. As Gwendolyn Hampton's case reveals, when untrained and needy female teachers become too involved with needy teens, misconduct can happen, misconduct that takes place right in front of administrators and teachers but is observed only by other students.

Thirty-two-year-old Gwendolyn Hampton earned respect as a seemingly devoted Spanish teacher, counselor, houseparent, and single mother at John Dewey Academy, a private boarding school for troubled teenagers in the small western Massachusetts town of Great Barrington.[5] But students and staff at John Dewey said they feel betrayed by Hampton after a federal civil lawsuit alleged that she had a secret sexual relationship with a student, Adam Helfand, and had at least one child by him. The relationship continued after Helfand graduated from John Dewey and attended college. According to Murphy, Hampton said, "I didn't believe I did anything wrong. I feel I was good for Adam at the time I had a relationship with him. I certainly wasn't luring or enticing anyone." Helfand, who was expelled from an Illinois high school in 1999 for using drugs and alcohol, was supposed to be getting help for his problems at Dewey. Instead, he said, Hampton gave him alcohol and prescription pills.

The civil suit accuses Hampton of "counseling malpractice." It alleges that Dewey Academy, its president, and its dean were negligent in failing to supervise Hampton. In her defense she said she developed a very close relationship with Helfand because she was asked to do too many things— teach him, serve as his primary counselor, and supervise him when he worked in the school kitchen. She often called him to her home to baby-sit or do chores and he became very close to her family. "The boundaries were blurred; I was his lifeline," Hampton said. Even now, Hampton in-sists she did nothing wrong and cared deeply for Helfand. "I didn't see myself going out with a kid," she said. "I brought out the best in him. He made grown-up decisions, mature decisions."

However, a sense of betrayal is still felt at the school, which is home to twenty-nine high school students, many of whom said their lives have been transformed by the program built on intense confrontational therapy. Matthew, a seventeen-year-old student, credits Hampton's counseling ses-sions with helping him give up his dishonest and manipulative ways and learn to tell the truth. "I feel as if she was very hypocritical," he said. "She did something that is almost unforgivable, that is very dangerous for the school. She didn't think of the consequences of her actions. She never fol-lowed her own advice." Diana Gittleman, a lawyer who teaches part-time at Dewey Academy, said that nobody had a clue. "It blows my mind because I think of myself as an intelligent and sophisticated woman," she said.

I believe Hampton's behavior is consistent with our profile. She felt she was good for Adam and was helping him, not trying to date a kid or lure him into a relationship. But as she reports, she became too involved as a teacher, counselor, and supervisor and formed a very close personal rela-tionship with Adam. As the relationship evolved her own need for such in-timate contact emerged, with Adam spending more and more time at her home babysitting and doing chores. The boundaries got blurred. Mischief happened. As her student Matthew suggests, she didn't think of the con-sequences or follow her own advice. Where was the supervision and mon-itoring by school administrators and colleagues? Clearly Hampton was crossing boundaries and heading for trouble. As Murphy reports, Hamp-ton's students were aware of her relationship with Adam. During one of the weekly confrontational group therapy sessions at the school, where staff and students gather in a circle, Hampton acknowledged being questioned about Adam's continuing visits after graduation and whether the relationship was appropriate. She responded, "I said he was having a hard time adjusting to college and I was supportive of him, which was true." Where was the training for Hampton to serve as a primary counselor and adviser and lead confrontational therapy, to be a lifeline for Adam? Was Hampton prepared for the demands of close contact with a student who was ten years younger than she? How much counseling and advising experience and training did she have to prepare her for this role? In the end she was charged with "counseling malpractice," suggesting that she either lacked effective training and counseling skills or chose to abandon them when her own needs became too powerful. Remember that Hampton was in her early thirties and Adam was in his late teens. In spite of the notions that "it can't happen here" and "no teacher should have such feelings," physical and emotional attractions can and do arise between teachers and students and can flourish without adequate supervision and intervention.

As this sad story reveals, it appears that Hampton was on her own, too involved in a close relationship, too needy herself, and operating without the necessary training, supervision, and monitoring to heed the red light of danger. No doubt she needed the confrontational therapy that students at Dewey had access to. Seemingly everyone was looking the other way except the students. As Diana Gittleman said, no one at the school had a clue, even when Hampton became pregnant.

I believe Hampton falls into the category of what researcher and psychologist Jane Kinder Matthews describes as teacher/lovers who fall deeply in love with the teenage student and need frequent validation from others. Matthews supports the major argument in this book when she suggests, "What you have is a needy child and a needy adult and many times, that's just abuse waiting to happen."

## THE CASE OF GARY JARVIS

Gary Jarvis provides probably the best example of what can happen when teachers become involved in close personal contact with needy students without adequate training, supervision, monitoring, and intervention. I became involved in chronicling Jarvis's story in 1993 when a *Newsday* headline caught my eye: "School Sex Abuse; Sachem High School Teacher Held in Case Involving Teens."[6] Jarvis was a neighbor of mine in Blue Point, Long Island. Although I did not know him personally, accounts by community members described him as a model husband and an excellent history teacher at nearby Sachem High School in Ronkonkoma, New York. But all that changed on June 24, 1996, when Jarvis was arrested for allegedly having sex at a motel with an underage student and fondling a fifteen-year-old student in a classroom. He was arraigned on a third-degree rape charge and a charge of third-degree sexual abuse, both involving students less than sixteen years of age. His neighbors were shocked. This was not the man they knew in the community. This case prompted me to write a brief fastback on teacher sexual misconduct for Phi Delta Kappa[7] in 1996, in which I briefly described Jarvis's predicament as well as the cases of Glenn Harris, Alois Vlhopolsky, and John Schaenman (also described in this volume). Jarvis ignored boundaries and became involved in risky sexual relationships with students that eventually led to the loss of his professional career, scorn by colleagues and community members, hurt and personal damage to his victims, and humiliation for his wife and family.

Jarvis, who was married without children, had been teaching in the Sachem school district for eighteen years. He successful in the classroom and earned tenure and had a positive evaluation every year. He was not a predator. He had no police record of past sexual misconduct. But, as Detective Lieutenant Robert Hoss of the Suffolk County Police Sex Crimes Unit said, "He was taking her to motels for sex. It was more than once or twice, maybe for about a year. He didn't drag her there." There appeared to be mutual consent between Jarvis and the student, a needy teacher and student finding each other and acting out right in front of the community. Jarvis's behavior presents the picture of an unsupervised teacher spinning out of control, not only risking taking a student to a local motel but on June 14, 1996, allegedly twice fondling one of his fifteen-year-old students who approached him in the classroom seeking consolation because her parents were vacationing on her birthday.

Police said Jarvis began his sexual liaison in the alleged rape case around May 1992. It ended and, Hoss said, and "she didn't want any part of him any more and I think he was running around looking for her in the neighborhood. 'Did you see so and so?' The parents after a while realized something was wrong." The father of the fifteen-year-old in the June 14 incident said Jarvis had taken his daughter to lunch in the past and made inappropriate sexual remarks. After the first hug the first day of the alleged fondling, Jarvis asked the girl if their lunch date was still on and reluctantly agreed to let her boyfriend come. "And he said to my daughter, 'It is time for a hug as we are friends again,'" the father said. "She reluctantly went over to him, and was afraid about what would happen, but since it was a teacher she went over to him."

After the second incident the daughter went to school authorities. The parents, on returning from vacation, called the police. School Superintendent James Ruck said that school officials initiated the investigation after a student approached the principal of Sachem High School South. Jarvis was suspended with pay and the police were called in.

The teenage girl Jarvis took to motels testified that they had intercourse and oral sex, which Jarvis videotaped and photographed during ten months in 1992, when she was fifteen and sixteen years old.[8] Suffolk County Assistant District Attorney Deirdre Creighton said, "He became her confidant." In her testimony the girl described how she lost her virginity to Jarvis, a father figure "who gave me attention he didn't give to other kids." The girl had grown up fatherless.

On July 18, 1994, Jarvis was sentenced to four to twelve years in prison. According to Smith, before imposing the sentence Suffolk County Court Judge Kenneth K. Rohl read aloud portions of letters sent to him by a Sachem schoolteacher and the superintendent of Sachem schools, urging prison time for Jarvis and saying his behavior had eroded public esteem for teachers.[9] "He has betrayed a public trust and has victimized young impressionable students," Superintendent Ruck wrote of Jarvis. An unnamed colleague of Jarvis asked the judge to make an example of him, saying, "This may in a small way help to lessen the loss of respect of parents and students for teachers."

Jarvis's case raises many questions and supports my profile of teachers at risk for sexual misconduct. For example:

1. Jarvis is seen by some students as a father figure, a confidant, who is easily available to offer consolation and support to needy students.

2. His relationship with the girl he took to the motel appears to be consensual. As Detective Hoss suggested, "He didn't drag her there."
3. His blatant acting-out behavior appears to go unnoticed by colleagues, administrators, and community members. He goes to the girl's neighborhood looking for her. He takes her to motels in the area. He videotapes and photographs the sexual acts. He hugs another girl in his class, takes her to lunch, and makes inappropriate sexual remarks.

Jarvis's behavior should have set off alarms for colleagues, administrators, parents, and community members. But there appears to have been an eerie silence, a looking the other way, as Jarvis plunged deeper and deeper into sexual misconduct and the margins of school life. Didn't anyone notice? Where were his fellow teachers? It appears there was none of the supervision, monitoring, or intervention that Jarvis needed. Boundaries were being crossed all over the place. And where was the training that might have helped Jarvis become aware of his own destructive needs and offered him a road map for help? Instead, as the letters to Judge Rohl suggest, the district's response was that Jarvis's behavior was an anomaly and out of character for Sachem teachers, suggesting that this type of behavior doesn't happen here. The message was that Jarvis was a bad apple and once he was gone, all would be well again. The message was that we don't need to train our teachers on how to establish clear boundaries when they become involved in close personal contact with students who are looking for a father figure, mentor, confidant, or consoler. Unfortunately the only lesson learned in Sachem seems to be that the problem was simply about Gary Jarvis, not about the teacher training, supervision, monitoring, and intervention process. This kind of response helped create a climate in which more teachers can follow in Jarvis's footsteps. Things stay the same. The only difference is that Gary Jarvis is gone.

## THE CASE OF GLENN HARRIS

It was a high school crush complete with love letters and teddy bears.[10] But it was not the kind of attention any parent would want for a teenage daughter. According to friends, Christina Rosado fell head over heels for her physical education teacher, Glenn Harris, 33, in 1994 and 1995 while she was a student at Creative Learning Community, an alternative high school in East Harlem in New York City. Her love apparently did not go unrequited. When her mother confronted Christina about the affair in early March, the girl and Harris disappeared together on a countrywide tour of cheap motels and amusement parks, stopping to inquire about marriage laws. Harris was charged with kidnapping. After a nationwide hunt for Harris and Christina, Harris surrendered to Edward Stancik, the special commissioner for investigations for New York City schools on May 16, 1995.[11]

Harris's case presented an opportunity to turn a spotlight on the ugly and mostly hidden problem of contact between school staff members and students.[12] Edward Stancik said, "I don't want people to think there are massive hordes of child molesters in the school but it is certainly true that there are lots of relationships betweens adolescents and school staff." Stancik also cites the case of Andre Cadet, a gym teacher who had a flagrant affair with a seventeen-year-old student. "They were holding hands in the hallway, hugging in the swimming pool. It was demoralizing for staff and students. However, after being charged Cadet was found not guilty of a criminal offense and given just a six-month suspension without pay." People in the system need to blow a very loud whistle when they become aware of sexual contact between and employee and a student. However, Harris came into the teaching profession with known problems. According to Russ Buettner, Harris was a former police officer who was asked to quit because of "attitudinal problems." He was a first-year teacher, beginning in September 1994, with no training or experience in working with needy adolescents in an alternative school environment. As the teaching year progressed, Harris ignored boundaries by making romantic gestures toward Christina during school hours, taking her out to lunch and dinner, giving her gifts, and exchanging love letters and notes. Not unlike the case of Gary Jarvis, Harris's behavior was ignored by colleagues and school administrators. Harris fit the profile of a teacher headed toward sexual misconduct without the necessary training, supervision, monitoring, and intervention, for the following reasons.[13]

1. The police said that the word of a Lolita-like relationship between Harris and the girl first surfaced among students and teachers in early October 1994.

2. At the school some teachers complained that the school administration was lax in dealing with the budding relationship. "The administration has a responsibility for the safety of the students," said one teacher there, who spoke on the condition of anonymity. "Appropriate measures were not taken."

3. Harris was often seen talking alone with the girl with the classroom door closed, strolling with her in Central Park, and asking her out for a birthday dinner.

4. Although Harris's actions toward students raised some suspicions, other colleagues and students described him as attractive and trustworthy. He was "not a guy you'd watch out for," a school official said. "This is a guy everyone trusted."

5. No formal complaint was lodged by the school until January, when Harris was transferred to Landmark School for "unrelated reasons."

6. Evidence of the romance came on March 7, when the girl's mother intercepted a letter her daughter had sent to Harris that was returned for insufficient postage. The letter clearly showed that the two were lovers.

7. After Harris fled with Christina, her girlfriends at school did not seem to be worried about her. "A lot of people in the class just think they ran away together," said Takiyah Tinsley, 14. "They thought they were going out together."

8. The Creative Learning Community, a school for underachieving or high-risk children, encourages friendships between students and teachers, teachers said, but it was clear to them that Harris, who was fresh out of graduate school, was crossing the bounds of propriety.

9. A neighbor of Harris, Desire Core, said he told her he enjoyed his job but "was a little scared about the young girl having a crush on him." She added, "We talked about that being normal for young girls with him being a good-looking older man and teacher."

10. When Harris surrendered to police on May 16, 1995, he justified his actions by painting himself as Rosado's savior. Harris said, "A student came to me with horrific tales of brutal family abuse that lasted years and years. Whatever happens, I hope someone steps in. She is a beautiful person and deserves respect."

Harris's story depicts what can happen when an untrained, inexperienced, and problematic teacher is placed in a role that encourages friendship between teachers and students. Harris took on the role of savior and friend, and that led to a love relationship was known to students who felt "they were going out" and to teachers who felt the administration "failed to take the appropriate action." Yet the administrators responsible for his supervision seemed to have either looked the other way or believed "this was a guy everyone trusted" and "not a guy you'd watch out for."

Harris himself had some concerns about young girls having a crush on him, which might have been responded to if the school had a training program for new teachers that focused on the real issues that these new teachers might face, such as how to respond when a student develops a crush. Such a concern might have come up in a supervisory session that encourages teachers to talk openly about issues that are often hidden, certainly not included in faculty room conversation. Yes, there is a lot of blame to go around. Colleagues could have stepped forward and confronted Harris when the administration failed to intervene. Administrators failed to provide the necessary safety and protection for Christina and intervention for Harris. In the end everyone in the school community lost because of inaction: students who now have to guard against close contact with teachers, teachers who feel let down by administrators who fail to act, parents who looked to the school to help their children and now find mischief instead, and administrators who failed to intervene when everyone in the school community knew a problem existed. But perhaps the biggest losers are schools like the Creative Learning Community that encourage close relationships between teachers and students but fail to prepare their teachers for such a role. Marginal students, like Christina Rosado, and their parents deserve better. They don't deserve to come into a new school that offers hope and opportunity and find themselves instead involved with untrained teachers who have no idea of how to establish professional boundaries and keep their personal needs separate. And they don't deserve the kind of school in which administrators fail to look out for their welfare and quickly address a teacher on the way to trouble.

## THE CASE OF DR. D—ALOIS DLHOPOLSKY

Alois Dlhopolsky was known as "Dr. D" at Holy Trinity High School in Hicksville, New York. The science teacher spent extra time with students if they needed help with physics or chemistry and was a teacher they would talk to about personal problems.[14] When a sixteen-year-old student had trouble with her boyfriend and her parents at the end of 1991, she turned to Dr. D for guidance. By May 1992 he was calling her at home and a month later they started "hanging out in school together" and he would drive her to his home in nearby Lindenhurst. There, according to Salcedo, they had sex.

But it wasn't until three years later that the former student, now nineteen, came forward to report the encounter to police. Dlhopolsky was fired from the school in February 1996 and charged with statutory rape; he maintained his innocence. According to his lawyer, Joseph Caramagno, Dlhopolsky "apparently had known the girl for a period of time. He maintained a friendship with her after she graduated. He denies any sexual involvement. It's the kind of thing that could happen to any teacher. I guess his mistake was being friends with her at all."

However, Drew Biondo, the district attorney, said there was nothing in the investigation to indicate the young woman had any reason to come forward other than the fact that she believed she had been wronged. In her statement to the police, the young woman said, "I always felt what happened was wrong and that if I didn't have the problems to talk to Dr. D about this wouldn't happen. I started thinking if this was my kid, this wouldn't be right." But according to Salcedo, other students were angry that the school fired Dr. D simply on an accusation. One student, Dale Thomas, said, "Everybody knows she would go there for extra help. Dr. D was a great guy. He'd come to our plays; he'd come to sports night. He never propositioned anybody, he never came on or anything like that." In February 1996 Dlhopolsky accepted a plea bargain.[15]

Here is yet another teacher who fits the profile of a teacher at risk for sexual misconduct. It's not simply that "his mistake was being friends with her at all," as Caramagno stated. Rather, it's about Dlhopolsky crossing boundaries and taking on the role of friend, counselor, and, it appears, lover. He sees no red light of danger. He calls her at home, hangs out with her at school, takes her to his home, and presumably has a sexual relationship, a close relationship that appears to be well known to students at Holy Trinity. As student Dale Thomas said, "Everybody knows she would go to his room for extra help." Yet while "everybody knows" there is no mention of supervision, monitoring, or intervention to help Dlhopolsky before he gets into trouble and loses his job. Where were his colleagues and the administration? This is a Catholic school with strict behavioral guidelines. Didn't anyone notice this relationship other than the students? And where was the intervention to help the young woman solve her personal problems before she moved into this risky relationship? Remember the words of Dr. Ava L. Siegler, director of the Institute for Child, Adolescent, and Family Studies in New York City that any adolescent is vulnerable; they are all looking for someone to emulate and offer approval.[16] She says, "Yet psychologically, they may not be ready to deal with the consequences of physical and emotional intimacy." What we find repeated again in this case is a needy, untrained teacher who was "cool" and spent extra time with students, who was the one they would talk to about personal problems, connecting with a needy student who was experiencing trouble with her boyfriend and parents. Surely some adults in the school saw a dangerous situation emerging, but no one acted.

## THE CASE OF KELLY ANNE GALLIGAN

In reviewing cases of teacher sexual misconduct, I have found two themes that play a predominant role in almost every case, whether it involves a consensual relationship between a teacher and a smitten student or a predator teacher luring a student into unwanted sex. One overriding theme is the lack of supervision, monitoring, and accountability of teachers involved in such inappropriate behaviors. The other is the lack of intervention even when crossing boundaries and being too involved in close relationships with students is beyond question.

Kelly Anne Galligan, a teacher in Lisbon Falls, Maine, was accused of having sexual relations with a student she was tutoring. The case vividly points out the risks and hazards that can befall teachers who ignore boundaries. As reported by the Associated Press in March 1995, Galligan, a third grade teacher, had sex with a fourteen-year-old student she was tutoring "on a pretty regular basis" during the fall of 1993.[17] The boy said he "didn't think it was such a big deal" and that the sexual encounters took place in Galligan's apartment in a house she was watching for its owner and at the student's home while his mother and younger sisters were asleep in their upstairs bedrooms. Galligan was indicted in December 1993 of having sexual relationships with this boy and another teenager half her age. She was forced to resign from her teaching position.

How did such a vivid tale of a teacher's crossing boundaries and ignoring the red light of danger evolve? At her trial Galligan was described by her lawyer as a dedicated teacher who believed her job didn't end when she left the classroom. She spent many nonteaching hours tutoring students and helping steer them away from drugs. But clearly that prolonged time with students was risky for Galligan as well. The victim indicated Galligan bought him dinner at "nice restaurants," took him shopping for back-to-school clothes, and helped him with book reports and math homework. Galligan's journey into sexual misconduct is similar to that of other teachers involved in such inappropriate behavior. The tutoring relationship deepened into a friendship and finally they became lovers. The lack of supervision in the Galligan case resembles that in other cases of teacher sexual misconduct. For example, there is no evidence of any intervention by school officials or community members, although Galligan was seen in restaurants with the boy, in stores buying him clothes, and was known to be meeting with him in her home and his home to help with reports and homework, get-togethers that, as the boy said, "usually involved having sex." Galligan even allowed the boy to bring his friends to her apartment while they were high on marijuana and stay the night. In the end her behavior was finally noticed. Rumors began to circulate throughout the town that Galligan was having sex with teenage boys, rumors that prompted police to conduct a surveillance of her apartment.

As Deputy District Attorney Craig Turner suggested at the trial, "What had been a friendship developed into a romantic relationship." Nowhere in the Associated Press article is there any mention of school officials. Surely someone or some group in a position of authority in the school must have observed Galligan's behavior or heard rumors from colleagues, parents, or students. Lisbon Falls is a small town and people's behavior gets noticed. At the trial the boy admitted telling his friends about his sexual relationship with Galligan. They knew Galligan was not only his tutor but also his friend and lover. Teens talk and someone had to hear. But no one intervened or confront Galligan as she took more and more risks. A needy, lonely person used her teaching and helping role to find a human connection and a needy teenager who was also searching to belong. Clearly a boy who had sex with his teacher in his own home, openly kissed and held her in his backyard, all within feet of his mother, lacked supervision himself. Two needy people were allowed to go unsupervised.

On December 13, 1994, a judge ruled that the evidence presented by the prosecution that Galligan had made self-incriminating statements could not be used because a Lisbon Falls police detective who was a friend had tricked her into making the statements.[18] So while Galligan admitted the relationship on March 11, 1995, she was acquitted of the charge of sexual abuse.[19] Galligan's lawyer, Leonard Sharon, focused on a civil suit the parents of the boy had brought against Galligan, telling the jurors, "It sounds like it's about money to me." But the alleged behaviors didn't go away and Galligan lost her teaching job, her career, and her reputation.

# NOTES

1. Roberta G. Simmons and Dale A. Blyth, *Moving into Adolescence: The Impact of Puberty Changes and School Context* (New York: Aldine De Gruyter, 1987), xii, 304, 351–52.

2. Caroline Hendrie, "Experts Convene on Sexual Abuse by Teachers," *Education Week*, 9 April 2003, http://www.edweek.org/ew/ewstory/cfm?slug=30abuse.h22 (accessed 8 August 2004).

3. William Swiggart, Karen Starr, Reid Finlayson, and Anderson Spickard, "Sexual Boundaries and Physicians: Overview and Educational Approach to the Problem," Vanderbilt University Center for Professional Health, http://mc.vanderbilt.edu/root/vumc/php?cph&doc=742 (accessed 13 August 2004).

4. Caroline Hendrie, "Abuse by Women Raises Its Own Set of Problems," *Education Week*, 2 December 1998, http://www.edweek.org/ew/vol-18/14women.h18 (accessed 13 August 2004).

5. Shelley Murphy, "Teacher in Abuse Suit Defends Actions," boston.com, 14 September 2004, http://www.boston.com/news/local/articles/2004/09/14/teacher-_in_abuse_suit_defends_act (accessed 15 December 2004).

6. Ellen Yan and Robin Topping, "School Sex Abuse: Sachem H.S. Teacher Held in Case Involving Teen," *Newsday*, 25 June 1993, 3 (A).

7. William L. Fibkins, *Preventing Teacher Sexual Misconduct* (Bloomington, IN: Phi Delta Kappa Education Foundation, 1996), 11–15.

8. Estelle Lander Smith, "Teen to Testify at Teacher Sex Trial," *Newsday*, 6 May 1994, 25 (A).

9. Estelle Lander Smith, "Jail for Teacher in Student's Sex Abuse," *Newsday*, 19 July 1994, 4 (A).

10. Russ Buettner, "Teacher, Teen on the Run for Love," *Newsday*, 11 May 1995, 6 (A).

11. Carey Goldberg, "Manhattan Teacher Surrenders in Kidnapping of Teen-age Girl," *New York Times*, 17 May 1995, 1 (A), 4 (B).

12. Bob Herbert, "An Ugly School Situation," *New York Times*, 17 May 1995, 19 (A).

13. Carey Goldberg, "Nationwide Hunt for Teacher and Girl, 15," *New York Times*, 11 May 1995, 1, 8 (B).

14. Michele Salcedo, "Teacher in Rape Case Popular in School," *Newsday*, 22 February 1995, 7 (A).

15. Geoffrey Mohan, "Guilty in Teen Sex," *Newsday*, 22 February 1997, 27 (A).

16. Margot Slade, "Yes, Statutory Rape Is Still a Rather Big Deal," *New York Times*, 11 June 1995, 9 (E).

17. Associated Press, "Maine Teen-ager Testifies of Sex with Ex-teacher," *Boston Globe*, 9 March 1995, 26.

18. Associated Press, "Evidence against Teacher Barred," boston.com, 13 October 1994, http://nl.newsbank.com/nl-search/we/Archives?p_action=print (accessed 20 November 2004).

19. Associated Press, "Maine Third-Grade Teacher Acquitted of Sexually Abusing Two Teen-Age Boys," *Boston Globe*, 11 March 1995, 14 (Metro).

## Chapter Three

# Cases of Coaches Who Become Involved in Sexual Misconduct

In chapter 3 I will focus on cases that illuminate the risks involved in long-term, intensive, and close relations between educators and students, such as the kind that can develop when male faculty members coach female athletes. I provide a classic example of the mischief that can happen when I discuss the impact of the early 1970s Title IX legislation, which spawned a wave of new sports teams for young women. These sports teams were often coached by male faculty members who had no training in how to carry on close contact with young women, many of whom saw their coaches as adult role models and the key to athletic scholarships and admissions to prized colleges and universities.[1] However, school leaders and parents never saw the risks involved for teachers and students until cases of sexual misconduct began to emerge, often with the victims being vilified and accused of a vendetta against successful, politically connected coaches who were community icons.

Putting together a profile of coaches who become involved in sexual misconduct is not difficult. In many of these cases there are clear signals that coaches were crossing boundaries. Yet, as is often the case in sexual misconduct and a key lesson in this book, in almost every case administrators, colleagues, parents, and students failed to help the victims and the coaches involved. Here is a tentative profile of coaches who are at risk for sexual misconduct:

1. Many coaches are community icons. Their winning records make them a resource for the school district's positive public relations for the school and community's pride, often in a time of calls for budget cuts.

2. Because of their iconic status, coaches tend to be politically connected. They bring winning teams to the community, putting the community and its schools on the front page of area newspapers and television stations, increasing scholarships and college admissions for student athletes, and serving as a draw to bring new parents and their athletic children into the community all tend to provide the coaches with star status.

3. As such, they are often beyond reproach and not required to follow the same rules and boundaries as other educators. They, as these case studies suggest, are their own bosses and supervisors. They are free to roam and act as they choose, a dangerous mix.

4. As male faculty members they have had little or no training in how to coach and carry on close contact over a long period of time with female athletes. The advent of Title IX not only created many new coaching opportunities with female athletes but also presented inevitable accidents waiting to happen.

5. As in other cases of sexual misconduct, while the sexual misconduct of coaches was observed and known to the professional staff, parents, and students, there appears to have been little outcry to confront the problem. The modus operandi has been to look the other way, keep your mouth shut, and hope someone in authority will act.

6. Many of the victims of coaches' sexual misconduct are afraid to report the incidents to school officials or their parents. They tend to feel that they need the coaches' support to gain admission to colleges and scholarship aid. This is particularly true for impoverished students who lack resources to support a college education.

7. Victims and their parents who come forward are often vilified and accused of waging a vendetta or trying to ruin the professional careers and personal lives of dedicated educators. In some cases they also experience threats to stop the accusations. The lesson? We don't want to hear any more talk about sexual misconduct on the part of our coaches.

## THE CASE OF JOE SUTTON

Many cases of consensual sexual relations between teachers and vulnerable students involve educators who lead extracurricular activities, such as coaches. Male coaches involved with high school female athletes stand out as a particularly risky environment for both coaches and students. But we should not be surprised by this phenomenon. The Title IX law enacted in 1972 barring sexual discrimination in schools that receive federal money opened the gates for young women to participate in organized athletics. Participation in women's athletic teams rocketed from 300,000 to 3 million in the wake of Title IX, creating a need for thousands of new coaches, many of them men who had little or no training in how to work in close, prolonged contact with female students who often saw these male coaches as mentors to help them obtain scholarships and admission to select colleges and universities.[2] Some of these female athletes might have been prone to "go along" with a coach's sexual advances because they needed their help to win a college scholarship.

Thus an attempt to solve a problem created a problem. As I observed as a high school educator and sports fan, in our efforts to create women's teams in basketball, lacrosse, softball, tennis, track, volleyball, and so on, the pattern in many schools was to hire male coaches who were already on staff coaching football, baseball, and so on, and with little or no training or orientation, announce that a program for female students was in place and let the games begin. In a sense the male coaches, already bonded and members of the school's coaching fraternity, took over the emerging women's athletic program. Don Sabo, a sociology professor at D'Yourville College in Buffalo, New York, attributes the predominance of male coaches in the wake of Title IX to various factors, including an upswing in male applicants for jobs that did not previously exist or did not pay as well as they did now, and a bias by some male athletic directors against hiring female candidates. In today's high school athletic programs, men coach the majority of women's teams.

But there is a dark side to the male dominance of women's athletic teams. In the wake of Title IX what really happened was that school officials and beleaguered athletic directors planted the seeds for mischief and sexual misconduct. School officials and athletic directors failed to consider the human aspects of male coaches, many of them in the twenty- to thirty-year-old age category, becoming involved with adolescents who were beginning to explore their own sexuality. Before the public hugs of congratulation after games escalated to private embraces in a school-room, Amanda Henderson said she found it flattering that a veteran high school football coach would take such an uncommon interest in her, a sophomore basketball player. Henderson recalled that the coach, Joe Sutton, refused to let anyone else tape her ankles before her games at Indian Land High School in North Carolina and, to the vexation of her female basketball coach, did not want anyone else around when he taped them. He never missed Henderson's games, chose Henderson as his student aide, and showered her with gifts like the basketball T-shirts she collected. During softball season, when he served as assistant coach, he parked himself at third base, her position, and supervised her every move. Henderson thought he wanted her to be a winner. But, she said, he gradually began to demand a dividend for his devotion. The hugs and compliments were followed by invitations to spend time with Sutton away from school. Henderson's parents became suspicious and eventually mobilized a school board investigation that resulted in Sutton's resignation in January 1998.

It was not a pretty picture for either Joe Sutton or Amanda. But again, we should not be surprised. Don Sabo suggests there is a special relationship between athlete and coach and "it's all about emotions, about trust and about the body. And when scholarships come into play, it's about money, too." And both the Joe Suttons and the Amanda Hendersons of the world can be victims. Clearly there is more opportunity for female athletes than ever before, but the flip side is that there is more risk to both coaches and athletes because we haven't developed effective training, supervision, monitoring, and intervention programs that would have enabled school officials, the athletic director, fellow coaches, and colleagues to quickly intervene to help Joe Sutton before he proceeded to cross boundaries. Dr. Joel Fish, director of the Center for Sports Psychology in Philadelphia, observes, "When you put a male into a position of power where he can manipulate something of real meaning to an athlete, such as playing time or scholarships, then add in the possibility of a young girl who may have a crush, you've got an extremely dangerous mix."

Sutton's connection to Henderson had destructive consequences for both. Henderson, accused of exaggerating Sutton's overtures, was ostracized by her teammates. The school board investigation of Sutton turned up complaints that he had committed indiscretions with at least four other students.

There are many lessons to be learned from this case. First and foremost is that school officials and colleagues, while observing inappropriate behaviors such as Sutton's taping of Amanda's ankles in privacy, often don't come forward to sound the alarm. Why didn't the female basketball coach speak out about her concerns? Where were the fellow coaches who observed Sutton's apparent preoccupation with Amanda at softball games? Why didn't teammates and other students speak out when they observed Sutton's special attention to Amanda and instead ostracized her for "exaggerating" Sutton's attention? As Edward Stancik, the special commissioner of investigation for the New York City schools, suggests, "This kind of sexual misconduct is a problem, not a pretty one, that must be faced and solved."[3]

## THE CASE OF RICK LOPEZ

Sexual misconduct doesn't just happen. As the case studies in this book demonstrate, sexual misconduct most often occurs in an environment that allows professional caregivers such as teachers and coaches to operate on their own, without guidelines, clear boundaries, training, supervision, and intervention. Those in positions of authority, whether they are administrators, teachers, parents, or community leaders, don't take notice or, when alerted to possible sexual misconduct, turn the other way. The turning away process is not always intentional and clear-cut. Rather, the process of choosing not to speak out and confront sexual misconduct is subtler and more confusing for the observer. As shown in many of these case studies, otherwise concerned professionals, parents, and citizens often mistrust their own initial observations and reactions; they feel that this kind of behavior can't be happening in their school and community. They may have long-term relationships and allegiances with the professional involved and they may lack the skills and sometimes the courage to confront such behavior.

Clearly Title IX, with all its good intentions, provided fertile territory for sexual misconduct to take place and allowed other adults to avoid the necessary intervention. The checks and balances to prevent misconduct were not in place in many schools. Untrained coaches were suddenly thrown together with aspiring female athletes who saw the coaches as their tickets to stardom. The coaches described in this chapter are not predators or evil people. They were male teachers following the same script they used for male athletes. What they didn't foresee was the possibility of physical and emotional attraction with these female student athletes, nor did they have the skills in how to set in place boundaries that might serve to protect them and their students from misguided and hurtful sexual relationships. Coaching female athletes was different and required a different script.

As I already suggested, Title IX opened up a broad frontier for secondary school and college female athletes. Junior and senior high schools throughout the United States began fielding teams in basketball, soccer, volleyball, tennis, softball, gymnastics, golf, field hockey, and so on. Often the coaches hired were males who already served as coaches for male teams in football, basketball, golf, wrestling, baseball, tennis, and so on. They knew the school system and the bureaucracy, had experience as winning coaches, and knew the ins and outs of helping their athletes gain admission and scholarships to major college and university athletic programs. Many coaches used their positions of power to become politically connected with influential community members through the use of booster clubs that financed parts of the athletic programs that lacked funding, such as new stadiums, uniforms, trips, publicity, and so forth. Their role and position of power was akin to a small-town mayor. Doors closed to others were open to them and their athletes. They were stars in their own right, a "somebody" as the saying goes.

These winning and politically savvy coaches understood that an important part of their task was to create the same liaisons with college coaches that they had made with their male students; that is, to literally sell their newly developed women's programs and student athletes to the highest bidder—colleges and universities that could offer the best scholarships and playing opportunities and be a springboard to life as a professional player in sports like basketball, soccer, and tennis. Many coaches understood that in addition to coaching, this kind of "selling" was the key to continuing their position of power in the school and community. The bottom line was that the community respected not only the number of games and championships won on the playing field but also the number of female athletes winning scholarships and prized college admissions. The bigger the numbers, the more secure their position. They knew that survival depended on greasing the relationship between the school and college admission officers, coaches, and travel team and summer tourney guru coaches. Coaching was just one part of their powerful position. Successfully selling their products to the highest bidder was as important. The tremendous rise in women's basketball at the high school and college level became the major vehicle for showcasing the emerging female stars, stars who would go on to fill the the collegiate ranks.

They showcased their talented female athletes by establishing a liaison between their star athletes and the so-called traveling teams or clubs that play on after the regular school season local, state, and even national club leagues and tournaments and at the growing number of year-round camps and workshops led by coaching gurus with a national reputation who acted as headhunters on the lookout for players with the potential to star at the college level. For some gifted high school athletes the season never ended. It was no longer about girls having fun playing high school ball. It became a year-long process that involved constant practicing, playing, doing well, getting noticed, getting one's name in the paper, and being helped to create a polished, professional-sounding résumé and videotape that could be forwarded to any interested coach. Yes, many parents were heavily involved, giving up their own personal lives and resources to make sure their aspiring athletic children had access to tournaments, camps, and workshops, settings that offered the best hope of landing a spot with a Division I team, which represented the highest achievement for many student athletes.

But in the process many parents found they were giving up more than time, resources, and unconditional support. If their student athlete was gifted, they often found that the gurus who coached and administered the traveling teams, tournaments, and camps would begin slowly but firmly to take over the lives of their children. The coaches demanded that the parents let the child spend more and more time with them so they could compete for scholarships, college admissions, and notoriety. The coaches also encouraged their student athletes to abandon the social aspects of high school life and involvement with peers. In a sense it was an informal contract between the guru coach and the parent and child, a contract that suggested, "If you want to get ahead and get to Division I, you do what I say. I am in charge, not you or your parents. I'll do all the thinking. Your job is to listen to me. I'll show you how to get better and get to where you've always dreamed of being. The crowds, the notoriety, the scholarships are there. Listen to me and me alone. The days of high school fun are over. This is work and serious business." So as the dark side of Title IX ran its course, many young women abandoned their friends, their teenage lives, the fun part of sports, and even their parents. They joined a select group of other female athletes in a cultlike environment led by the guru coach. It was a family whose sole purpose was to outperform others. They became like their gifted male counterparts, always future oriented, preparing and learning how to sell themselves to the highest bidder. The fun days were over.

What are those summer camps and tourneys like for high school students who are college hopefuls? Dozens of college coaches were seated at courtside during a July 2003 game between the Colorado Hoopsters and the Minnesota Metro Stars at the Clackamas Community College gym in Oregon City, Oregon.[4] These were two traveling teams made up of star high school basketball players. The coaches present represented colleges and universities from some of the biggest names in women's basketball. Winter recruiting helps, but coaches wanting to take their teams deep into National Collegiate Athletic Association (NCAA) tournaments needed to get top players seen, not heard, in gyms such as this one. Notre Dame's Muffet McGraw and Stanford's Tara Van Derveer joined Colorado's Ceal Berry and Chris Denker of Colorado State on the two rows, one at each end of the court. They were separated from the rest of the crowd because NCAA rules forbid contact between college coaches and the girls' summer club coaches. There were also coaches from other schools such as Dartmouth, Xavier, Lafayette, Maryland, and Vanderbilt. Many of the coaches start their summer recruiting here with four hundred coaches watching 159 teams. The girls' summer circuit is booming. The tournament started in 1979 with eight teams. Maryland coach Brenda Frese calls this kind of summer tournament "one hundred times better" than what she sees watching high school teams in the winter. "High school? Ugh. I can't even stand to watch high school ball to be honest. It's not the same level. It's not the same intensity. A majority of these summer players have a level where they can play whether it's Division I, II, or III."

But these summer tourneys have pitfalls for high school athletes. Bill Saum, the NCAA's director of agent, gambling, and amateur activities, suggests that there is almost no oversight compared to high school basketball. "The goal here is to encourage the recruiting process to be moved into the high school, so our coaches can deal with the high school coaches, high school administrators, and the families of the players. These people clearly have the best interest of the student-athlete in mind. It's an academically based environment. They're around these kids for reasons more than basketball."

But the reality is that the college coaches profit from these summer tourneys, which allow them to see a large number of players in a short time. And that is not about to change. The gurus, like Rick Lopez, who coached the Colorado Hoopsters until 2003, will remain powerful figures in the lives of aspiring women basketball hopefuls. Dr. Joel Fish's "dangerous mix" was created as Rick Lopez and his Colorado Hoopsters gained national prominence as a basketball training site that could pretty much guarantee any woman basketball player automatic access to a college scholarship and stardom. That is, until Lopez was charged with having ongoing sexual relationships with some of his players and committed suicide on December 26, 2004, at 12:22 A.M.

Here is the dark side of Rick Lopez and how he ruled his players and, as Joel Fish suggested, used his position of power to manipulate some of his players into sexual relationships. Rick Lopez was not a trained educator like others in this book but he represents the growing involvement of guru coaches who are attracting naive, vulnerable high school female athletes under the guise of guaranteeing scholarships and in the process controlling and isolating them from their parents, friends, and community life. His story and the evolution of the Colorado Hoopsters into a national training ground for future university and professional basketball players reveals how guru coaches such as Lopez have infiltrated high school sports and in many cases taken over the college recruiting process, relegating high school coaches, administrators, and the families of players to minor roles reducing or eliminating the once powerful position of "those people who clearly have the best interest of the student athlete in mind. They're around these kids for reasons more than basketball," as the NCAA's Bill Saum explains.

Lopez's story will help us understand the risks involved in abandoning our children to gurus whose powerful and unchecked positions can lead them to cross boundaries and become involved in sexual misconduct. His story and the story of the Colorado Hoopsters remind educators that their prized student athletes are vulnerable to paying a price for stardom, a price that can cost student athletes a sense of who they are as individuals, their dignity, and trust in adult mentors who are controlling, manipulative, and seductive. They pay a price that makes them want to go back in time, wish they were kids again, had stayed home and played ball with their home team, hung out with their friends, didn't wander too far from their families and teachers and didn't become "somebody." As this case suggests, becoming "somebody" can cost gifted student athletes a lot, especially if they don't have an advocate in their corner to guide them through the dangers.

Let's begin the story of Rick Lopez by clicking onto the Internet site for the Colorado Hoopsters, www.coloradohoopsters.com.[5] What strikes you first is the list of "Class of 2005 Commitments" by star players to schools such as Duke, Minnesota, and Brown. There are also links including media associations and promotional resources, a list of current players, application forms for membership, lists of upcoming leagues and tournament schedules, and successful alumnae playing at the college level. It's a flashy page that includes the name of the coach who replaced Rick Lopez as director of coaching. He is Steve Fendry, a three-time Division II All-American as a player at Western State College and girls' coach at Mullen High School in Denver, where he guided the school to three straight Colorado state championships (2001, 2002, and 2003) and was named Colorado 4 A State Coach of the Year in each of these seasons as well as Colorado Girls' High School Coach of the Year in 2001 and 2002. The page indicates that "a few of Fendry's former high school players in the college ranks include Lacy Shafer (Clemson) and Kelly O'Connell (Cal Berkeley)." One can sense that this is a big deal. And it was Rick Lopez who made the Hoopsters a big deal.

An article in an October 2003 *Denver Post* series about Rick Lopez, "Lopez: Hoopsters Not about Money," suggests that "the Colorado Hoopsters are Rick Lopez's life."[6] They also provided his livelihood. Lopez drew his only income from the Hoopsters. He charged his fifty-eight players $100 each month, a gross salary of $29,000. Junior high girls practiced year-round with the Hoopsters; high school players participate for about five months between high school seasons. Parents also pay Lopez up to $5,000 to cover their daughters' airfare to tournaments as well as meal and room costs on the road. The Hoopsters spend almost all of July traveling to tournaments. For some low-income players, Lopez has personally paid their travel bills. Briggs indicates that Nike, which sponsors twenty-five girls' club teams across the United States, does not pay Lopez but for nine years the shoe giant has given the Hoopsters free shoes, bags, and uniforms. Mary Thompson, who runs Nike's All-America Basketball Camp and handles the Hoopsters' sponsorship deal, says, "The Colorado Hoopsters name speaks for itself all over the country."

Since the early 1990s Lopez estimated his traveling team of suburban all-stars had racked up eighteen tournament titles. According to a 2003 article, "Success a Constant Among Lopez's Teams," his teams barnstormed through fifty game seasons losing once or twice, whipping some opponents by seventy points, and luring dozens of college coaches to their games.[7] Yet Lopez had been panned for his abrasive tactics and haunted by sexual innuendoes involving the coach and some players. According to Briggs, Lopez denied any inappropriate contact with players. Even hardcore critics said the guy could coach. As for the players, Tarah La Par, a University of Wyoming freshman, says, "We're all sisters. Rick preaches about being sisters on the team. So when we are on the courts, you trust one another. You win together." Lopez had held just two tryouts in the past decade and never recruited. He didn't have to, according to Briggs. Parents and their daughters flocked to the Hoopsters on their reputation for winning national tournaments and earning college scholarships. Lopez estimated that more than 100 of the 250 Hoopsters he had coached went to college for free.

But not everyone was happy with Lopez's harsh coaching style. Practices, which put raw junior high talents against high school stars, could run as long as four hours and often included a verbal thrashing for mistakes. Lopez's harsh behavior was often difficult for some parents who sat by silently as Lopez hurled basketballs and dirty words at their children.[8]

Randy Sutton, whose daughter Kelsey played for the Hoopsters in the late 1990s, recalled, "Your kid would get yelled at or screamed at or degraded. We all hated him and didn't like what he was doing but we all let it happen." Parent Cecilia Studdard, whose daughter Katie played for Lopez in the late 1990s and 2000, suggested, "They, the parents, have bought into his whole story that their child will not earn a scholarship unless they play for him. Whatever he dishes out, they take." Some parents, like Jeff and Shelly Steig, began to feel like their daughter, Amber, didn't belong to a basketball club.[9] They felt like the entire family belonged to a cult. They admit to being lured into the program with the promises of a college scholarship but once inside the Hoopsters, the Steigs soon saw the bad—the punishments, the paybacks, and the atmosphere of fear that they say coach Rick Lopez used to control every corner of his program. That culture was further tainted by allegations of sexual contact between Lopez and some players, yet few families ever walked away from the elite program. When the Steigs decided to leave the team, Shelly Steig said several parents remarked to them, "Your daughter will never play again," while others wondered how they managed to walk away from this cultish setting. Keep in mind that Lopez had coached the past ten Ms. Colorado Players of the Year. Walking away was not easy, especially when most parents hated Lopez's aggressive behavior but chose to let it happen.

As we all know, when we allow ourselves, our families, or our children to be abused by others without raising an alarm, confronting the problem, or simply walking away, that signals the Rick Lopezes of the world to take even more freedoms, since they know they will not be challenged. They are in the driver's seat and calling out the orders. The student athletes and their parents become the followers.

Lopez raised the ante with his star players. Once he had complete control over the players and reduced their parents to observer status, Lopez moved into new territory—sexual relationships with some of his players. At first he denied any such conduct and called the rumors attacks on the Hoopsters program. Then, in 2003, three ex-Hoopsters accused Lopez of having or trying to have sexual contact with them and a fourth said she witnessed him having inappropriate contact with another player.[10] The players were eighteen years of age or younger at the time of the incidents. The four former players alleged that the acts occurred in Lopez's car, in a park, and in out-of-state hotel rooms in 1992 and 1993. Two of the players said they had ongoing relationships with the coach. One player recounted a series of sexual encounters she said she had with Lopez during drives to and from practices in the summer of 1997. She was fifteen at the start of the summer. He was twenty-four. The player said she stayed quiet at the time to secure a college scholarship. "The last thing you're going to do is come out and say this man did this to you when he holds the key to your future in his hands." However, after several meetings with representatives of the *Denver Post* in 2003 she agreed to come forward in order to "keep it from happening again."

Lopez denied all the charges but admitted spending the night at some players' homes. He said his stays were never improper and the player's parents always welcomed him. Lopez said his close friendships with several girls and their families fueled years of false perceptions and jealous rumors by other Hoopster parents and opposing coaches. Lopez denied any inappropriate physical contact with of his players. He acknowledged briefly dating one of the four when she was eighteen but disputed her statement that they had sex or that he was her basketball coach. No charges were filed.

However, Lopez's history of possible sexual misconduct with his players had been known for some time by law enforcement officials, school coaches who served as part of the feeder system that directed star athletes to the Hoopster program, and star athletes and their parents. In fact, Lopez's behavior had been examined three times. In the mid-1990s the Boulder County Sheriff's Office investigated Lopez's association with the then fifteen-year-old who has since talked to the *Denver Post*. At that time she told detectives she had no contact with the coach. No charges were filed. Several years later an anonymous caller contacted the Highland Ranch Middle School, where the Hoopsters practice, and raised concerns about the coach. The school administration looked into those concerns but found no reason to change their rental agreement with Lopez. In the summer of 2003 the Douglas County Sheriff's Office interviewed Hoopster parents, current players, and former players about Lopez but reported that they had "no credible evidence at this point."

In the summer of 2003 Lopez was still supported by many parents who discounted the rumors as gossip. "Parents make up stories and it's pure downright jealousy," said Barbara Walters, whose daughter Keirsten starred for the Hoopsters in the mid-1990s and later played at the University of Connecticut. Lopez continued to accuse opposing coaches of generating sexual innuendo about him as a ploy to shut down his program and steal his players. He suggested that the rumors about him had circulated so long that some people started believing them. However, he indicated that "maybe it's time for me to move on." The *Denver Post* ran a series about Lopez in October 2003 that included allegations of possible sexual misconduct. He remained with the team until July 30, 2004, when he abruptly left the team in the middle of a tournament in Oregon.

On July 30, 2004, Lopez was arrested and charged with fifty-five felony sex assault charges and four misdemeanor charges for having sex with three players who were minors.[11] He was held on $500,000 bail in the Douglas County Detention Center in Colorado after being arrested in Syracuse, New York, while trying to visit a former player who had pressed charges against him. During a preliminary hearing in December 2004 a judge found enough evidence to hold Lopez for trial. He committed suicide on December 26, 2004, by hanging. Lopez had threatened suicide in tapes made in July 2004 of phone calls between him and one of the players he allegedly assaulted. He also apologized to one girl on the tape about the alleged incidents. Chris Denker, head women's basketball coach at Colorado State, where several former Hoopsters have played, called the apparent suicide Lopez's final crime and said it robbed ex-Hoopsters and victims of a choice to heal through the legal process. "The whole thing about Rick going back to day one, he was selfish. He showed his true colors by ending it like this, rather than showing any true remorse about the kids. He showed no remorse. The players wanted a chance to put some finality to the situation through whatever the proper process is. Now they're not going to have the opportunity."[12]

Yes, suicide was on Lopez's mind. Ironically Lopez had used the threat of suicide to prevent parents from taking their daughters out of the Hoopsters program. Threatening suicide seemed to be his last way to control his players, his final move as a coach, and his final move in life. He didn't want to lose—games, players, parental support, tournaments, and close relationships. Here was, it seems, a needy guy who used his coaching skills and domain to draw vulnerable teenagers and parents into his controlled world so he could become a "somebody" on the national scene. But in his search for affection he allowed himself to abuse the trust and faith of his players to satisfy his own sexual and emotional needs.

Reporter Bill Briggs was right about Lopez when he reported, "The Colorado Hoopsters are Rick Lopez's life." Now it became "were" his life. Could an early intervention have saved him and his victim athletes? Clearly the answer is yes. People knew but few—parents, players, feeder school coaches, or administrators—spoke up. As Jenny Cook, a former Hoopster and now the girls' coach at Golden High School in Colorado, observed, "I would never send any of my kids his way. I don't think it's a very healthy environment." But perhaps the best reason that there was little public outcry about Lopez's behavior lies in the words of one of his victims.

An incident in 1992 involved Lopez and one of his players kissing and petting in his car on a dark street near her home, culminating in unwanted intercourse. In recalling the relationship the young woman said, "I didn't know how to react. I wish I had known to say no, but I didn't know what to do. It was so awful I just froze into nothing." She added that after the so-called relationship ended, she was contacted by a Boulder County Sheriff's Office detective but revealed nothing about her relationship with Lopez. She said, "I remember thinking I am not signed with a college basketball program yet; even if I don't play for Rick, I don't need Rick hating me, because Rick knows a lot of college coaches." This victim, like many members of the Hoopsters organization, didn't know how to react and didn't know what to do. Plus, as she suggests, even after the angst of the relationship she believed, like many others, that Rick Lopez still held the keys to open the doors to college admissions and scholarships. The result? Like the victim described here, they "just froze into nothing."

Rick Lopez was surely part of the problem of hustling female student athletes but he wasn't the cause. He got caught up in the hype of winning, as did his student athletes. In the end he represents a special kind of sexual misconduct that is evolving with the pressure on young men and women to perform as miniprofessionals in the hands of guru coaches who, like Rick Lopez, have their own problems. The case of Rick Lopez was a tragedy for himself, the Hoopster players, their parents, and the high school coaches who sent their best student athletes into harm's way. A process that promised fame and fortune through sports also included serious personal risk. Their normal reactions to possible danger were blurred by dreams that someday these student athletes would be wearing the green uniform of Dartmouth, the purple of Xavier, the brown of Lafayette, or the gold of Vanderbilt. Their radar was turned off. Think for a moment what might have happened if the parents, students, and high school coaches had acknowledged the signs of danger in Lopez's program and acted aggressively. Sounding the alarm and walking away might have led Lopez into some kind of intervention.

Coach Jenny Cook did act. As she said, "I would never send any of my kids his way. I don't think it's a very healthy environment." Clearly we need more Jenny Cooks if we are going to solve the problem of sexual misconduct in women's athletics. In the end Rick Lopez's victimized students were denied closure because of his suicide, but so were he and his family.

There are many lessons to be learned from the Rick Lopez case and the saga of the Colorado Hoopsters. Here are some examples:

1. We need to educate professional staff members—teachers and coaches—parents and students to beware of gurus and saviors who promise fame and fortune but have their own personal agendas. They need to recognize the danger amid the glory involved in sports.
2. We need to create school environments that offer ongoing training, supervision, and intervention to teachers and coaches involved in long-term close contact with students, particularly male coaches with female students.
3. We need to create a school and community-wide helping network in which professional staff, students, parents, and community members are alert to possible sexual misconduct and are encouraged to act and not freeze.
4. We need to closely examine student, parent, and professional staff relationships with organizations outside the school that may damage students.
5. We need to teach our students that walking away from a hurtful and perhaps destructive situation, albeit sponsored with good intentions, is an appropriate choice.
6. We need to teach our students, parents, professional staff, and community leaders that there can be a downside to excelling in sports.
7. We need to raise the awareness of school district leaders—superintendents, principals, athletic directors, coaches, guidance counselors, and PTA presidents—that it can be harmful to use gifted athletes as merchandise and public relations tools to sell their communities and colleges and universities on the success of their programs and promote both the athlete's and district's success by encouraging participation in unregulated and unsupervised out-of-school programs over which the district has no control.
8. Finally, as the NCAA's Bill Saum suggests, we need to advocate a recruiting process for student athletes that is "led by high school coaches, administrators, and families. Those people who clearly have the best

interest of the student athletes in mind. They're around these kids for reasons more than basketball."

## THE CASE OF THE SOUTHINGTON HIGH SCHOOL GIRLS' BASKETBALL AND SOFTBALL COACHES

In some school settings there is a climate that turns a blind eye to predatory sexual misconduct by a group of teachers and coaches in spite of ongoing rumors of such behaviors in the school community. These are school settings in which a powerful group of predators has taken over and been given free rein to prey on vulnerable students without fear of detection. It appears such was the case at Southington High School dating from the late 1970s through the late 1980s.

Southington is a picturesque New England community located twenty miles from Hartford, the state capital. The town has many churches and civic groups. In the 1970s and 1980s the high school had approximately 1,700 students in grades nine through twelve. The community had a great interest in the schools and successful athletic programs, including the emerging interest in girls' sports at the high school level that began in the mid-1970s. For many in Southington, this was the best of times for girls' high school sports.[13] Southington High School's 1981–1982 girls' basketball team captured the school's first-ever girls' basketball championship under coach Joseph C. Daddio. The same year, the girls' softball team, led by coach Joseph J. Piazza, won its fourth state championship in five years. The girls' teams were a community treasure. Their victories were the talk of street corners, bars, and beauty salons, and their back-to-back championships catapulted the already popular coaches and their teams to new levels of prominence. The success of the Southington High's girls' teams was well publicized and the players were devoted to the male coaches who brought them that fame. However, twenty years later the public would learn that there was a seamier side to the girls' sports teams. At least a dozen former players from that period have told police that Daddio, Piazza, and some former assistant coaches, including Raymond Acey, Bob Shirley, and teacher William McKernan, had sex with them and others or made inappropriate sexual overtures or both. The popular coaches and teacher were all married and in their late twenties or early thirties at the time the incidents allegedly occurred. "These guys were famous in town," said a former basketball player, who added that her relationship with one of the assistant coaches in the late 1970s involved kissing and petting. "Everyone was thrilled that our girls' teams were winning. The feeling was that the coaches couldn't do anything wrong. You'd never think of challenging them on how they behaved." Another woman who claimed she had a sexual relationship with Daddio in the mid-1980s said, "At the time I thought the attention was a good thing because I thought it meant the coach had noticed me and it would benefit the team." And as one woman who played softball and basketball in the early 1980's and said she had a sexual relationship with Acey observed, "We grew up watching the Southington High School teams before us win state championships and we dreamed of having the same opportunities. Girls did not have the opportunities they have now. Times were different. A coach making a pass at you was not something you told anyone about."

How did a group of girls' basketball and softball coaches become involved in sexual relationships with their players in such a close-knit community for such a long period of time without intervention? This was not a case of one coach acting as a predator. There were five coaches involved. And these five coaches used a variety of threats to keep their victims silenced, threats that appear to have worked for many years. Two former Southington High School female basketball players talked of losing their virginity to coaches, while other female athletes described coaches making sexually tinged comments, rubbing their legs, and kissing them.[14] They told police that the coaches took advantage of their positions as trusted mentors to pursue sexual relationships. Those are among the allegations of misconduct involving several high school coaches and more than a dozen female athletes from the mid-1970s through the 1980s that were described in a police report released in early January of 2002.

The men accused were former high school teacher and girls' basketball coach Joseph Daddio; former middle school teacher and assistant basketball coach Raymond Acey; high school math teacher, softball coach, and former assistant high school basketball coach Joseph Piazza; middle school science teacher William McKernan; and former assistant basketball coach Robert Shirley. All denied any wrongdoing except Shirley, who could not be located.

The police report summarized an investigation launched in October 2000 that was prompted by a complaint from a woman who did not want her niece in a class with Daddio. The woman told police that about twenty years earlier she had sexual relations with Daddio in his home, her home, and a local motel. Daddio submitted his resignation as a business education teacher on October 13, 2000, after the former student came forward. He was accused of having sexual relations with two students and engaging in inappropriate behavior and contact with at least two others.

Acey resigned the following month after similar allegations against him surfaced. He was accused of having sexual relations with two students, making sexual comments to another student while he was her coach and later, after she graduated, developing a sexual relationship with her, and counseling many girls in his locked classroom. Piazza was placed on administrative leave following release of the report. He was accused of having a sexual relationship with a former student that started several weeks after she graduated, having a sexual relationship with another student, touching one student in an inappropriate manner, and having inappropriate contact with players. During the police investigation a number of women came forward, many saying they knew their basketball and softball teammates were having sex with coaches and some coaches, including Piazza, had intimate relationships with multiple students. Shirley, a volunteer assistant coach, was accused of having a sexual relationship with a student during her junior year. The police report indicated that he provided alcohol for her and let her stay overnight at his apartment. As part of the police investigation one woman described herself as Shirley's "project." She was sixteen and Shirley was thirty when she lost her virginity to him. Afterward Shirley told her that she would be "blackballed" from colleges she wanted to attend if she ever told anyone about their relationship. Shirley's whereabouts remain unknown. McKernan was accused of kissing an eighth grade basketball player on the lips several times at after-school events and telling her that he would kiss her for every block she made on the court. The team's three female chaperones accused McKernan of touching players during basketball drills and telling them how romantic he was. He was placed on paid leave in January 2004 but was returned to teaching and coaching with only a reprimand. School officials defended their handling of the 2002 complaint against McKernan, saying the evidence wasn't strong enough.[15]

However, as in many other cases of sexual misconduct, the reaction of the community was split. Residents and former players rushed to defend the coaches, blitzing local newspapers with letters to the editor and questioning the validity of the women's complaints. One former player who came forward said, "Instead of the community jumping to the support of victims, they have gone straight to asking these former female student athletes why they waited twenty-plus years to tell their stories. Why don't they ask the teachers and coaches why they have not yet come forward to confess their sins?"

A January 14, 2002 *New York Times* article entitled "Town's Disgust Outlasts a Statute of Limitation" reported that in the aftermath of the police report released on January 8, 2002, there was a high level of disgust in Southington, particularly that the coaches involved could not be charged because the statute of limitations for prosecuting such contact is seven years.[16] There was also hostile reaction by some community members to the news that William McKernan was simply reprimanded and allowed to stay in the classroom and resume his coaching duties. As the *Times* reported, George DiBattista, who had lived in the town for thirty years, said, "No one should get away with that and these guys are still getting a pension and everything." Matthew Welinsky, whose daughter was a student at Southington High during the 1980s, said, "It's a black eye on the face of the town. You think you can trust teachers and that your children are safe and then you hear about something like this going on without anyone knowing it." An editorial in the *Hartford Courant* on June 4, 2004 echoes the community disgust by stating that Mr. McKernan should have been removed from coaching, given the complaint and the ample evidence of a culture of permissiveness in the athletic department. "A virus isn't curable but it should be contained."

There are many lessons in the Southington case. Here are some examples:

1. Coaches who have outstanding athletic teams can slip into predatory behavior with their team members. They have been promoted to a place of prominence in the community and feel they have no limits or boundaries. Absent training, supervision, monitoring, and intervention, successful coaches, not unlike the highly successful professionals like Plass and Shockro, can become renegades preying on innocent victims. Early training, supervision, monitoring, and intervention might have

saved the careers of Daddio, Piazza, and Acey and brought about changes in the behavior of Shirley and McKernan.

2. Many adults in leadership roles in the school surprisingly state they had no indication of the sexual misconduct of the coaches. School officials during the time of the alleged incidents admit to being equally surprised by the allegations, insisting they saw no hints that anything was wrong. "Absolutely not. I never knew anything about it, and if I had, I would have done something," said David Larson, a former assistant superintendent. Former athletic director Dominic D'Angelo also said, "Absolutely not. I never heard of any reports of any misconduct on the part of coaches. I had never had a complaint." Corine Lorenzet, who headed the high school guidance department, had no comment. In the police report one woman said she told Lorenzet just a few years ago about a sexual relationship between Daddio and her sister. The woman told Lorenzet about the relationship because she wanted her son removed from Daddio's class. According to the report the student was removed from Daddio's class but the allegations were never investigated. Someone in authority had to have known. As parent Sharon Dinsmore, who had two daughters who played high school basketball in the 1980s, said, "There were rumors around. I certainly heard them. I believe a lot of people were aware of the possibility of impropriety and didn't pursue it."

3. Close contact between coaches and players that lasts over long periods of time can be risky when coaches are not trained in how to carry on such behaviors without crossing boundaries. Clearly no red light went off for Daddio, Piazza, and the other coaches.

4. High school athletes who are victims of sexual misconduct may be threatened into holding their silence because of their need for recommendations for college scholarships from the same coaches and teachers who are abusing them. As one former student said, "I needed to play ball. I wanted to get some scholarship help because I knew my parents couldn't afford to send me to school for four years. I went along with the relationship." The increased pressure on high school students to get a leg up on admissions to name colleges and secure scholarships may act to silence students who are victims of sexual misconduct. They may "go along," naively trusting that the abuse they are enduring will have a happy ending, buoyed by the words of coaches and teachers who promise scholarships and early admissions.

5. The coaches involved in their predatory activities focused on players with parents who either were inattentive to their comings and goings or, like most, believed their daughters were in caring, responsible hands with their coaches. A former player who claimed she had a three-year relationship with Piazza that was limited to kissing and hugging said, "We did not dare tell our parents or anyone else, as we knew our parents would never allow us to play for Southington High and the coaches again." Another former player said, "My parents would have killed me if I went to them. And I don't think anyone at school would have believed me."

6. As in other cases of sexual misconduct, victims who do come forward often are not believed and are subjected to hostile reactions in both the school and the community. They are often perceived as troublemakers out to undermine community icons and the reputation of the school. The result? Make the victims suffer so that other victims are afraid to come forward.

## THE CASE OF DAN MARINO

In early November 1999, forty-four-year-old Dan Marino was a star teacher. He was the coach of the boys' football team, assistant coach of the girls' lacrosse team, and gym teacher at New Hyde Park High School, one of the high schools in the Sewanhaka Central High School District in Nassau County, New York. His football team had just won the Nassau County championship. He was an icon in the community, someone the students, parents, and community members looked up to, a professional who was guiding New Hyde Park athletic teams into county and state prominence.

His iconic status changed on November 10, when Marino was suddenly transferred to teach gym at another school in the district because of allegations that he had an improper relationship with a female student.[17] Jean Fichtl, a school board member, said, "Dan Marino was transferred to break the connection to a student with whom district officials believe he had a voluntary, one-on-one relationship. The transfer is the strongest action that the district could take because the school had limited evidence."

Marino's first reaction to the transfer was not unlike those of other teachers whose sexual misconduct becomes known. His response, according to

Kreytak and Sarra, was, "Rumors are rumors. They can really hurt a good man and his family." Marino was married with two children. However, school officials challenged the credibility of his response by indicating they believed a seventeen-year-old senior girl had a close relationship with Marino in which the two spent extended periods of time together off campus. Marino was fired as football coach two days before New Hyde Park's regular season finale, a game the team won to finish with a record of 7-1. His record in fourteen seasons at New Hyde Park was 87-27 and he led the school to the conference title game three times in the 1990s.

The Sewanhaka High School District's response to alleged sexual misconduct was not unlike that of other school districts to such behavior. They transferred him to another school. As school board member Fichtl said, "To remove a teacher under tenure is very difficult." And remember, Marino was a community icon. He had taken his football team to three conference title games in the 1990s and won the coveted title in 1999. When he stated, "Rumors are rumors. They can hurt a good man and his family," perhaps he was sending a message that he held a position of power in the community and he was not going quietly. The investigation proceeded and, according to Kreytak and Sarra, while the district's union leaders were ostensibly backing Marino and saying his employment was not in jeopardy, the union contract allowed the school board to vote to begin proceedings to fire a teacher under several circumstances, including "engaging in conduct unbecoming a teacher" and "moral turpitude."

In the end the allegations of sexual misconduct against Marino were found to be true. In early March 2000, he was arrested and charged with statutory rape of the girl, a felony punishable by up to four years in prison. The police charged that Marino and the seventeen-year-old had consensual sex in September 1999, at the Sunrise Motel in nearby Lynbrook.[18] Although he was arrested for that one incident, according to police it was believed that the sexual encounters happened more than once as they often met off campus and during the summer months. Yet Marino served no jail time. Marino admitted he carried on a sexual relationship with the girl from February 1999 until his arrest in March 2000, four months after school officials suspected something was wrong.[19] Marino's lawyer, Brian Davis, said, "This was an aberrant occurrence. He's not a predator. This has never happened before." Marino was placed on probation for three years and forced to resign his teaching position and surrender his New York State teaching license.

There are many lessons to be learned from the Dan Marino case. Perhaps lawyer Davis is right when he states that Marino was not a predator and this was an aberrant occurrence. But Marino was at risk of becoming involved in crossing boundaries and sexual misconduct. The conditions for such activity were present. For one, the relationship began in February 1999, when Marino became assistant coach of the girls' lacrosse team. Here was a man whose entire coaching experiences were with male students. Did he have any training to prepare him to work with female students in the close relationships required in coaching? And what abut his own personal needs? Yes, he was married and had two children. But did he have unmet personal needs? I know from my own experience as a high school educator and sports fan that football coaches spend a great deal of time away from their families, holding practices, scouting and watching films of coming opponents, meeting with college recruiters, and often seeking relief from the pressure to win games by hanging out with fellow coaches to socialize. It's a clubby atmosphere that often does not include wives and serves as a home away from home for overextended coaches. Coaching then can spawn a negative home relationship in which wives and children are increasingly left on their own, even abandoned, and marriages become at risk.

We don't know about Dan Marino's home life, but when he became involved as a girls' high school coach he ignored professional boundaries and the warning light of danger ahead. He met with the girl for extended periods of time off campus during the summer months and eventually risked having sex with her in a local motel. He appears to have been blinded by the relationship and was perhaps naively confident that his power role as football coach left him free to pursue such risky behavior. Yet someone had to notice. Weren't there fellow coaches, girls on the lacrosse team, colleagues, administrators, or parents to observe a successful professional and a love-struck teenager headed for trouble? Clearly there was enough evidence, although the school board's initial reaction was to say there was "limited evidence," although they had reason to be suspicious.

Here was a highly successful teacher who went down a wrong road and ended up ruining his career and harming a vulnerable student, his wife, and his two children. Training, supervision, monitoring, and intervention might have saved Dan Marino from this tragic end. Training might have alerted colleagues and fellow coaches to their responsibility to quickly confront a teacher moving beyond professional boundaries and guiding him to credible sources of help, particularly a teacher like Dan Marino who was a star in the district and may have begun to believe that boundaries, rules, and regulations didn't apply to him. One of the major lessons from the Dan Marino case is that coaches may be the most vulnerable group to sexual misconduct when training, supervision, monitoring, and intervention are absent. All the conditions for sexual misconduct to occur exist in the world of the coach—a close relationship based on trust and mutual respect, developed over a long period of time and where the personal needs, hopes, and lives of both players and coaches are shared. It is a club-like atmosphere in which loyalties, commitments, and the ceremonies involving winning and losing are special and often kept secret. It's a "home away from home," "we're in this together," "us against the world" situation where, as in the case of Dan Marino, caution is sometimes thrown to the wind.

## THE CASE OF JOHN SHOCKRO

John Shockro was a popular teacher and coach for twenty-seven years at Old Rochester Regional Junior and Senior High Schools in Mattapoisett, Massachusetts. However, Shockro had a dark side to his personality. He sexually assaulted a number of young women during his career. In 2003 he pleaded guilty to seven counts of child rape and six other sexual assault charges involving two students from 1994 through 1996. At least eight more students and ex-students were waiting to testify to their similar abuse but the hearings never went that far.[20]

How did a popular teacher, coach, and coordinator of the town's recreation program pursue his predatory behavior without intervention by the school committee, administration, colleagues, or community leaders? The Old Rochester school community is relatively small: 2,700 students from the towns of Marion, Mattapoisett, and Rochester, with a population of 15,000 residents. These are tight-knit communities where people are known to each other. The school administrators and school committee turned a deaf ear to the wails of the injured children, and the system put in place to protect children betrayed them, valuing sportsmanship, political ties, and the usual tendency to victimize the victims in such cases over truth and the grim reality that John Shockro was a pervert. Why is it that otherwise responsible adults enabled Shockro to prey on young women unhindered and stood by him throughout the trial intoning his good character, community service, and total inability to commit such abominable acts? Where were the training, supervision, monitoring, and intervention that might have helped John Shockro avoid such damaging and dangerous behaviors early in his career? Where was the intervention for many vulnerable young women? Why were they unable to raise their voices and be heard?

I believe one of John Shockro's victims provides answers to these questions.[21] Teachers who are predators, like Shockro, often seek out students who are undergoing great stress, need adult attention, can be intimidated by threats, are less likely to be believed, and in the end are easy marks and low risks. During Shockro's trial the teenage girl talked about trust, betrayal, and the pain of a community that refused to believe her report, a school that turned its back on her. The teenager who told school officials in 1995 that the junior high gym teacher raped her said she was shunned by friends and community members who all rallied behind that longtime basketball coach when the allegations were made. She said nearly everyone in town was convinced she was lying and that the brain tumor she suffered made her delusional. "Two out of 6,000 people believed me," she said. "My self-respect turned into self loathing. Nobody would believe Coach Shockro would do this. Abuse isn't supposed to happen in a town like ours." Only after a second victim came forward, followed by eight more, did some people begin to believe what she told school officials the year before. The second victim, who was just thirteen when first sexually assaulted by Shockro, said she was a vulnerable girl befriended by a man admired in both the community and the school. His attention was flattering but when the attention turned to sex, it was frightening, she said. Both girls said they were the ones who shouldered the blame when the allegations were finally made public. They said other students called them whores and liars. One girl attempted suicide and wound up in a trauma hospital.

Fortunately some adults did believe these young women and were able to intervene and offer a lifeline of support. One of those adults was Detective Mary Lyons of the Mattapoisett Police Department. On February 7, 1997, Lyons sat behind a one-way mirror at the South Bay Mental Health Center in Plymouth, Massachusetts, and listened to Shockro's sixteen-year-old victim detail three years of rape and sexual assaults.[22] From that day she began a fact-finding odyssey that uncovered a town secret whispered about for years. Soon after hearing from the first victim she learned the name of another teenager raped by Shockro. As word spread about the investigation, calls began coming into the police station. There were more victims. Some left names. Some left phone numbers. Some left other information. Lyons became an investigative team of one in a case that divided the town between believers in the children and believers in the coach, who wore white ribbons to show their support. In the end eight young women agreed to testify in the case to back up the two teenagers' allegations, strikingly familiar stories of being seduced by Shockro. Gentle words and friendship were followed by kisses and then rape in the locker room, his office, and his beach house. The rape often involved punching the girls if they resisted. Where were the school officials charged with ensuring these young women's safety? Who knew what—and when?[23]

One of the victims, who was sixteen at the time of the attack in the boys' locker room, told high school athletic director Joao Rodriguez about it the following day. According to the police Rodriguez accompanied the girl to a female guidance counselor and at some point an assistant principal was made aware of the allegations. Old Rochester Regional High School Principal James Eagan said in February 1997 that his staff took appropriate measures at the time and that school officials who heard the girl's report firsthand in 1995 did not believe it fit the description of a crime. But there is more to this story. School officials seemingly chose to protect Shockro rather than the young woman. Maureen Boyle reports that Detective Mary Lyons indicated that the teenage victim and her parents had pressed complaints about Shockro to school officials but had been told to stop talking about the rape and Mr. Shockro or face disciplinary action or suspension. And while school officials knew about the incident, it was not reported to the Massachusetts Department of Social Service or police, as required by law. Meanwhile, Shockro was reprimanded with a written warning from Superintendent Walsh.[24]

As Detective Lyons observed, "People had to know. Maybe they didn't say anything because there was no proof. Maybe they didn't want to believe it." A lot of people knew. Some of the girls who were teenagers twenty years ago were still in town. The people who "knew" included athletic director Joao Rodriguez, junior high principal Robert Gardner, guidance counselor Barbara Meehan, assistant high school principal Carol Stigh, high school principal Eagan, assistant superintendent Carol Young, and superintendent Walsh. Where were the training, supervision, monitoring, and intervention Shockro so desperately needed? Instead, Shockro was treated as a deity and left to act out. As Detective Lyons said, Shockro's standing in the community provided a cloak of immunity and respectability. "He was with the in crowd," she said. "He was an icon in the community." He was a good father, family man, and churchgoer, involved in youth activities. He was a star in the school and the community and often stars begin to believe in their special status and ignore boundaries. And where was the intervention for Shockro's victim? The young woman and her parents came forward with a story of a rape in the locker room and she was threatened with suspension. Shockro's profile was not hard to read.

This case demonstrates how we all, including Old Rochester educators Gardner, Rodriguez, Meehan, Stigh, Eagan, Young, and Walsh, can be blinded by our allegiance and trust in our star teachers even when the red light is flashing for all to see. Chances are that Shockro was asking for help as he took more and more risks by having sex in his office, locker room, and beach house. Chances are he wanted to be caught. He probably knew that some colleagues, administrators, students, and community members were aware of his destructive behaviors.

Ignoring or allowing John Shockro to continue his sexual misconduct came at great cost to the reputation of the Old Rochester school district, the district's top management team, the professional staff, and community advocates and watchdog groups. But probably the most painful example lies in the professional censure of junior high principal Robert Gardner, who retired in 1997. Gardner should have a plaque and letters bearing his name adorn the auditorium at Old Rochester Regional High School, where he was principal for three decades.[25] Instead Gardner asked school officials to scrape his name from the wall after fresh allegations were released that he had ignored complaints about gym teacher John Shockro, who pleaded guilty in 1997 to raping two students. Over Christmas 2004 officials planned to quietly remove Gardner's name at his request. But the question of whether he should be honored still divides residents of Marion, Mattapoisett, and Rochester. Some believe Gardner should be honored for his long career. Others say any memorial to his service would become an indelible reminder of one of the region's most wrenching episodes. "Gardner has a legacy and it shouldn't be on the auditorium, because it will just remind people of the injustice done to girls over time," said Dede Smith. "The school didn't do its job when Gardner was at the helm."

In addition to not doing his job, Gardner viewed female students as suspect and given to fantasizing about sexual relationships with staff. He also swept aside Shockro's own statements that he kissed, hugged, and swore at his victims. According to Levenson, Gardner testified at Shockro's trial that he did not know that one of Shockro's victims, Kristen Canty, had alleged she was raped in 1996. He said he only knew that Shockro had kissed her, hugged her, and swore at her. Gardner told the court that he believed many high school girls were "a different breed of cat" and he believed Canty was fantasizing. Even after another student came forward in 1997 with concrete evidence that Shockro had sexually assaulted her, Gardner did not revisit Canty's allegations. He testified instead, accepting Shockro's assurances, that "nothing untoward" had occurred.

Gardner's response to a petition by community residents to remove the plaque was, "I have been the designated sin-eater for the past ten years and I am really tired of it. It's just too much." So the Old Rochester School and the community remains divided over who knew what and when. Questions still abound. Community resident Cathrene Foren of Marion suggests that if Gardner "had a glimmer of what was going on, that would be tragic." The one constant in he revelations about Shockro has been the testimony of former students at the school. Hearing their assessment leaves little doubt that, as Kathrene Foren and Dede Smith suggest, "The school didn't do its job when Gardner was at the helm. A former student of Shockro described his behaviors. "He set up an office in the boys' locker room," said a thirty-nine-year-old former student. "Girls used to visit there at lunchtime and all kinds of crazy stuff. They shouldn't have been in there." It's too bad the leaders of the Old Rochester schools didn't have that wisdom. "They shouldn't have been in there," says it all.

As we have seen in this chapter, coaches who are community icons with powerful political connections are often given a pass on their conduct. And administrators like Gardner who have their own bias toward female students, such as his view that high school girls were a different breed of cat and subject to fantasizing, are stuck with their narrow-minded perceptions, which, as in the Shockro case may prevent them from serving *all* of their students. Clearly Shockro needed training and early intervention that might have gotten him the help he needed. Gardner also needed training to explore his own biases toward female students and also in how to intervene when he became aware of students in his charge being abused. Like Shockro, he had nowhere to turn for help. Yet he had to have had a glimmer of what was going on. Shockro told him he had been kissing and hugging his students. Other students came forward with accusations of sexual misconduct by Shockro. One wonders if he told anyone—his wife, his children—of his concerns, or was he the prototypical good soldier, protecting his troops to the end, even when they were far off course. Three decades as an educator in which he probably offered countless hours of help to thousands of students ended in disgrace because of allegiances and flawed, noninclusive perceptions about female students. The bottom line is that he didn't trust what the students told him. How long had he held that view? Training would have helped explore that dark side of his administrator persona. In the end personal allegiance and perceptions prevented his acting to shine needed light on the dark shadow of sexual misconduct. He too was victimized by Shockro.

## THE WASHINGTON STATE STORY OF COACHES' SEXUAL MISCONDUCT

This final section on coaches' sexual misconduct borrows on the yearlong research of *Seattle Times* reporters Christine Willmsen and Maureen O'Hagan that culminated in a series entitled "Coaches Who Prey," which ran in December 2003 and January 2004.[26] In my view their study supports many of the aspects of my sexual misconduct profile for coaches at risk. The data also documents how some educators involved in unchecked sexual misconduct move on to adopt a predatory lifestyle and prey on vulnerable students while believing they will not be challenged, confronted, or fired, cases and issues I discuss in chapter 4 on teachers as predators. Their findings focus primarily on identifying and getting rid of coaches involved in such behaviors rather than, as I suggest, adding on the necessary and important piece of providing ongoing training, supervision, monitoring, and intervention. If we are to solve the problem of sexual misconduct by coaches and teachers, we need to take the next step and train coaches how to set boundaries and carry on close contact with vulnerable teens while at the same time being aware of their own vulnerability and risk of sexual misconduct and how to seek intervention when needed. Willmsen and O'Hagan's research offers a clear picture of the problem and the kinds of variables, like the advent of Title IX, that helped to create such misconduct. Here is what they found.

Willmsen and O'Hagan report that over the past decade, 159 coaches in Washington have been fired or reprimanded for sexual misconduct ranging from harassment to rape. Nearly all were male coaches involved with female students. At least ninety-five of these coaches continue to teach or coach. The number of offending coaches is much greater because, when faced with complaints against coaches, school officials often failed to investigate them and sometimes ignored a law requiring them to report suspected abuse to police.

Even after being caught, many men were allowed to continue coaching because school administrators promised to keep their disciplinary records secret if the coaches simply left. Some districts paid tens of thousands of dollars to get coaches to leave. Other districts hired coaches they knew had records of sexual misconduct. The research also focused on the growing field of club teams, such as the Colorado Hoopsters I described in the Rick Lopez case. They found that coaches could get a job or start a team with almost no regulation or oversight. They also found that many parents ignored the warning signs of sexual misconduct. As in the Rick Lopez case, some parents suspected misconduct and did little to stop it, trusting the coaches while doubting their accusers. As Willmsen and O'Hagan report, "Unfortunately, everyone has an investment in the silence, the parents, the team and community," said Sandra Kirby, a Canadian sociologist who studied sex abuse of athletes by coaches. "The measure is, if a coach has had good successes, that's all they worried about. They're ignoring the victim." The research also points out the demand for quality coaching in girls' sports that burgeoned when Congress passed Title IX, requiring that girls be given the same educational and athletic opportunities as boys.

The number of girls playing high school sports in Washington tripled since 1972. In 2002 43 percent of high school girls played sports. That doesn't include the thousands of girls who take part in recreational and club teams outside the school setting. The boom created a nearly insatiable call for coaches, most of whom were men, coaches whom Willmsen and O'Hagan describe as being in a demanding profession with long hours, often low pay and pressure from insistent fans. And for most of the more than 20,000 coaches in Washington State, the reward is the satisfaction of mentoring student athletes, not only in the skills of a particular sport but in the values of teamwork, practice, and sportsmanship. And as I argue, Willmsen and O'Hagan suggest that there is a potential downside to such close contact that can span many years. They point out that coaching presents a unique opportunity for sexual misconduct. Coaches work with athletes for hours at a time, often over several years, in unstructured situations such as locker rooms or out-of-town tournaments. Kids and parents generally admire them. But the research of Willmsen and O'Hagan shows that Washington teachers who coach are three times more likely to be investigated by the state for sexual misconduct. As New York City investigator Stancik might suggest, maybe 195 plus coaches out of 20,000 is not an epidemic but it is a problem that must be solved.

However, what is most compelling about this research are the examples of what can happen to coaches when they cross boundaries without training, supervision, monitoring, and intervention. As in the cases of Joe Sutton, Rick Lopez, Dan Marino, and John Shockro, many of the coaches were, as O'Hagan and Willmsen suggest, "big celebrities,"[27] who at first became involved in sexual misconduct and then moved on to adopt a predatory lifestyle as coaches because they were allowed great leeway, for example, by moving from school district to school district and from one victim to another. Let's examine the case of Randy Deming, a successful wrestling coach in Blaine, Washington, who won state coach of the year honors in 1990. When district officials suspended the coach in 1990 for allegedly rubbing a student's breasts and touching her genital area, people circulated petitions asking the school not to terminate him. The school district charges against him were dropped when he accepted an offer to resign in March 1991. Still, he went on to coach at Mount Adams White Swan High School, which wanted a top wrestling coach and hired Deming in 1995 despite his background, according to O'Hagan and Willmsen. However, Deming didn't change his troublesome conduct. Girls there complained of unwanted touching. Mount Adams officials disciplined him five times in the 2002–2003 school year. In March 2003 he was charged with two counts of fourth degree assault with sexual motivation after allegedly touching two eighth grade girls in his math class. After a three-day trial jurors decided the coach's conduct was not criminal and acquitted him. Meanwhile, the Mount Adams school district gave Deming notice that he was going to be fired. He is appealing that decision and is on paid leave.

Then there is the case of Port Townsend basketball coach Randy Sheriff. As O'Hagan and Willmsen recount, the bond between a fifteen-year-old Port Townsend girl and the thirty-four-year-old Sheriff was especially strong. The girl, raised in a troubled home, saw Randy Sheriff not only as a mentor but also as a surrogate parent and "the greatest dad in the world." Sheriff showered her with attention, then with flowers and chocolates, then with kisses. Before long the coach, a married man with two children, was sending the teenager love notes. By the time she was sixteen, she says, they were having sex in his car, at his house, and in motels. She babysat his two children, was Sheriff's coaching assistant for the boys' basketball team, and accompanied him on road trips. She trained with him at his California basketball camp and he took her to Australia with an adult men's team. The girl reported, "I felt puzzled, like I was falling in love. He was my lifeline." According to Heather Carter, a Port Townsend graduate, "Everyone in school knew they were having an affair." Although the Port Townsend school officials believed Sheriff was having an intimate relationship with her, according to Willmsen and O'Hagan they simply nudged him out of town, allowing him to land a coaching job in the Cascade Mountain town of Cle Elum, where he was accused of preying on another girl. The girl sued the Port Townsend district and they settled with her for $50,000 in 2002. Sheriff settled for an undisclosed sum and was told he was no longer needed as the boys' basketball coach despite taking the team to the state tournament. Why was Randy Sheriff allowed to cross boundaries? As Heather Carter suggests, "everyone knew." One reason is that Sheriff came to Port Townsend in 1983 with an impressive résumé. He had led Seattle's Roosevelt High School basketball team to the 1973 state tournament and played professional basketball in Europe. He was a star player and coach and as we have seen in this chapter, star coaches are often given great leeway. According to Willmsen and O'Hagan, Randy Sheriff still denies the charges.

According to O'Hagan and Willmsen, Detective Joe Beard, who is in charge of sex offender notification in the Snohomish County Sheriff's Office, said that school administrators, as well as parents, need better training in identifying and acting on signs of sexual abuse.[28] Beard is right, but his suggestion is only a partial solution to the problem.

Coaches and teachers need training to set boundaries and learn how to behave before they begin coaching athletes of the opposite sex. And clearly there are examples of female coaches being involved in sexual misconduct with male athletes and homosexual and lesbian relationships that must be put on the training agenda. And when coach–student relationships begin to develop into close friendships and have the potential for misconduct, clear avenues for help must be available for both the students and the coaches involved. Tim Flannery, assistant director of the National Federation of State High School Associations (NFHS), puts it well when he suggests, "The only way we can slow sexual misconduct down is to educate coaches on their role and responsibility. Training becomes critical. School and state associations should make it mandatory for coaches to get this training."[29]

As publications of the Women's Sports Foundation point out, romantic and/or sexual relationships between coaches and athletes compromise the professional integrity of the coach and the educational mission of athletics. The foundation suggests that coaches need to be provided with information, training, and continuing education about how power, dependence, "love," and sexual attraction can influence coach–athlete relationships. Upper-level administrators need to take responsibility for organizing educational and training sessions for coaches and staff. However, the Washington Interscholastic Activities Association (WIAA), which oversees athletics in the state's nearly three hundred school districts, has not addressed sexual misconduct in the clinics its member coaches are required to attend. "The association tells coaches how to tape ankles, prevent injuries, motivate athletes, even deal with the media, but not how to keep proper boundaries with young players." There is work to be done to ensure that coaches and teachers receive the kind of training they and their students deserve.

In chapter 4 I will present cases of sexual misconduct that involve predator teachers, professionals who clearly set out to lure vulnerable students into unwanted sexual acts to satisfy their own emotional and sexual needs. As these case studies demonstrate, predator teachers are not difficult to identify. Think about the cases of Randy Deming and Randy Sheriff that Willmsen and O'Hagan so vividly describe. "Everybody knew," including administrators, teachers, students, and parents. Predators lure students into relationships often using the guise of mentoring and coaching. But these kinds of predatory acts are different from those I have identified as consensual between a teacher and student and those that may be a by-product of an intense coach–athlete relationship. Predatory relationships are not rooted in friendship and love. There is no bonding, caring, or deep relationship in these cases; rather, they involve only using, threatening, and damaging the victims. Perhaps Randy Deming and Randy Sheriff, two highly successful coaches, could have been helped if they had been confronted early on and received the necessary supervision and intervention to turn their lives around. Maybe that could have spared them a predatory life, always moving from town to town, victimizing more students, being found out, dismissed, or fired and then beginning the predatory pattern all over again. And maybe their victims would have been spared the humiliation and shame. As Port Townsend graduate Heather Carter said, students "snickered" when Coach Sheriff and his victim disappeared into a room off the gym. Everyone knew, and when everyone knows it can be humiliating for the victims. They are no longer students or kids. They are trapped in an adult world where, as the victim observed, "I felt humiliated and puzzled."

Deming and Sheriff are not indicted but, as Willmsen and O'Hagan suggest, they operated on their own without boundaries and at a dreadful cost.

## NOTES

1. Robin Finn, "Growth in Women's Sports Stirs Harassment Issues," *New York Times*, 7 March 1999, 1 (A), 24 (L).
2. Robin Finn, "Growth in Women's Sports Stirs Harassment Issues."
3. Edward Wyatt, "Schools Show Jump in Reports of Sex Abuse," *New York Times*, 23 May 2001, 1, 7 (B).
4. Adam Thompson, "Summer Tourneys Where It's At for College Hopefuls," DenverPost.com, 12 October 2003, http://www.denverpost.com/Stories/0.1413.36%7E76%1680740.00.html (accessed 2 January 2005).
5. Colorado Hoopsters, *News & Announcements,* January–February 2005, http://coloradohoopsters.com (accessed 2 January 2005).

6. Bill Briggs, "Lopez: Hoopsters Not about Money," DenverPost.com, 12 October 2003, http://denverpost.com/Stories/0.1413,36%7E76%E1692617.00 .html (accessed 2 January 2005).

7. Bill Briggs, "Success a Constant among Lopez's Teams," DenverPost.com, 12 October 2003, http://denverpost.com/cda/article/print/ 0.1674.36%7E76%7E1690741.00.html (accessed 2 January 2005).

8. Bill Briggs, "Coach's Harsh Style Brings Success, But Some Wonder If It's Worth It," DenverPost.com, 12 October 2003, http://denverpost.com/cda/ print/?0,1674.36%7E76%7E1690925.html (accessed 2 January 2005).

9. Adam Thompson and Bill Briggs, "Cult of Personality," DenverPost.com, 12 October 2003, http://denverpost.com/cda/article/print,0,1674.36%7E76% 7E1692763,00.html (accessed 2 January 2005).

10. Adam Thompson and Bill Briggs, "Sex Charges Shadow Girls' Coach," DenverPost.com, 12 October 2003, http://www.denverpost.com/cda/article/print/ 0.1674.36%7E76%7E1693470.00.html (accessed 2 January 2005).

11. DenverChannel.com, "Girls' Basketball Coach May Face 100 Counts Related to Sexual Assaults," 20 August 2004, http://www.thedenverchannel .com/print/3669544/detail.html (accessed 2 January 2005).

12. Arthur Kane, Adam Thompson, and Bill Briggs, "Coach in Sex Case Apparent Suicide," DenverPost.com, 12 December 2004, http://www.denverpost.com/cda/ article/print/0.1674.36%7E53%7E2620282.00.html (accessed 2 January 2005).

13. Mary Ellen Fillo, "Shadows Stalked Girls' Glory Days," Associated Press, 10 March 2002, 5–7 (A1).

14. Kimberly W. Moy and William Schubert, "Coaches Avoid Charges in Sex Allegations," Hartford Courant, 10 January 2002, 7 (A1).

15. Hartford Courant editorial, "End Mr. McKernan's Career," Hartford Courant, 4 June 2004, 10 (A).

16. Southington Journal, "Town's Disgust Outlasts a Statute of Limitations," New York Times, 14 January 2002, 17 (A).

17. Steven Kreytak and Gregg Sarra, "'Connection' Broken," Newsday, 11 November 1999, 5, 60 (A).

18. Steven Kreytak, "Gym Teacher Charged with Rape," Newsday, 8 March 2000, 8 (A).

19. Chau Lam, "No Jail for Coach in Affair," Newsday, 21 March 2000, 29 (A).

20. Mary Ann Sorrentino, "John Shockro Not the Only Guilty Party in Sordid Case," SouthCoastToday.com, 7 January 1998, http://www.s-t.com/daily/01-07-98/c04op105.htm (accessed 8 November 2004).

21. Maureen Boyle and Bridgette Sweeney, "From Trust to Betrayal and Lingering Pain," SouthCoastToday.com, 31 December 1997, http://southcoasttoday.com/daily/12-97/12-31-97/a011o0005.htm (accessed 8 November 2004).

22. Maureen Boyle, "Detective Lyons Investigated Shockro Case 'Relentlessly,'" SouthCoastToday.com, 8 January 1998, http://www.s-t.com/daily/01-98/01-08/a01o003.htm (accessed 9 November 2004).

23. Ellen O'Brien, "Police Press Questions to School in Rape Case," *Boston Sunday Globe*, 16 February 1997, 4 (B).

24. John Estrella, "10 Days of Allegations, Questions, and Headlines," SouthCoastToday.com, 23 February 1997, http://www.southcoasttoday.com/daily/02-97/02-23-97/a011o005.htm (accessed 8 November 2004).

25. Michael Levenson, "Ex-principal Rejects Naming Honor," boston.com, 12 December 2004, http://boston.com/news/local/articles/2004/ex_principal_rejects_naming_hon (accessed 12 December 2004).

26. Christine Willmsen and Maureen O'Hagan, "Coaches Continue Working for Schools and Private Teams after Being Caught for Sexual Misconduct," SeattleTimes.com, 14 December 2000, http://seattletimes.nwsource.com/news/local/coaches/news/dayone.html (accessed 11 January 2005).

27. Maureen O'Hagan and Christine Willmsen, "Misconduct Often Goes Unpunished by Districts," SeattleTimes.com, 15 December 2003, http://seattletimes.nwsource.com/news/local/coaches/news/daytwo.html (accessed 11 January 2005).

28. Maureen O'Hagan and Christine Willmsen, "What School Districts Can Do," SeattleTimes.com, 15 December 2003, http://seattletimes.nwsource.com/news/local/coaches/news/schools.html (accessed 11 January 2005).

29. Christine Willmsen and Maureen O'Hagan, "Misconduct Registry, More Training Needed for Washington Coaches," SeattleTimes.com, 16 December 2003, http://seattletimes/nwsource.com/news/local/coaches/news/state.html (accessed 11 January 2005).

*Chapter Four*

# Cases of Predator Teachers

As William Swiggart suggests in his study of sexual misconduct among physicians, there are four categories of offenders:

1. The lovesick physician, who may feel normal ethical guidelines do not apply in matters of love. These physicians appear healthy but may be experiencing significant life crises.
2. The limitless physician, with tireless and selfish devotion to patients, who may be vulnerable to the demands of difficult patients. This physician avoids conflict and has almost no ability to limit patients' requests.
3. The predatory physician, who represents small but notorious groups of physicians' misconduct cases often associated with severe narcissistic and antisocial personality disorders.
4. The psychotic physician, who represents the smallest group, is the truly mentally ill physician.[1]

Again, I believe Swiggart's categories are helpful in our study of teacher sexual misconduct. The focus of this chapter is on a small but notorious group of educators who appear to be predators and in some cases mentally ill. What is startling in these cases, as in the cases in chapters 2 and 3, is the lack of response by administrators and colleagues, even when students clearly observed that behavior was well out of the norm. These case studies demonstrate the need for administrators and teachers to look closely at the behavior of teachers who are at risk of harm to themselves and their students and not turn a blind eye.

93

I believe a review of these cases offers a beginning profile of educators who are predators or on the road to such damaging behavior. Here is my assessment of a beginning profile:

1. Predator teachers are not interested in consensual or love relationships with students. Their goal is to satisfy their own needs.
2. Predator teachers often seek out students who are undergoing great stress, need adult attention, can be intimidated, and are less likely to be believed if they cry out for help. These students are easy targets and at low risk to seek help.
3. Predator teachers use the threat of blaming the victim, brand the victim as the aggressor and a liar, and use physical force and intimidation to keep their victims in an abusive relationship.
4. Predator teachers can be powerful star teachers or coaches who are renowned in their school districts and are major contributors to the district's success and reputation. Their predatory behaviors, while known in the school and community, are allowed to go unchecked because of their powerful positions. Their student victims are thus reluctant to come forward and those who do are often not believed or are pressured to be silent.
5. Many predator teachers are allowed to transfer from school to school even though their predatory behaviors are known by the sender schools.
6. Predator teachers use their teaching, advising, and coaching relationships with needy students to lure them into sexual relationships.
7. Predator teachers have extremely risky behavior in that they become involved in sexual relationships with students in the school building and in their own homes.
8. Predator teachers are often reprimanded for their behavior but operate without the training, supervision, monitoring, and intervention needed to curb their misconduct.
9. In some school settings there is a climate that turns a blind eye to predatory sexual misconduct by teachers and coaches, in spite of ongoing rumors of such behaviors in the school community.

## THE CASE OF MICHAEL DWAYNE BLEVINS

Michael Dwayne Blevins was a teacher and coach in Wytheville, Virginia. In 1998 he was charged with sexually abusing three young women. One girl from Rural Retreat High was involved with him for more than four years, even after he left Wythe County for Shawnsville Middle and High School in Montgomery County, Virginia.[2] He became involved with two other seventeen-year-olds at Shawnsville. In each case he played on the girl's sympathy and then won greater access by asking her to spend extra time with him to enter statistics into a computer. At Rural Retreat the computer was in his private office in the high school wrestling room, while at Shawnsville it was in his apartment. "It was always, 'Poor me. I need all the mothering and comforting,'" said Sandra Wright, an assistant prosecutor in Montgomery County, one of the three counties where Blevins pleaded guilty to sex charges. "And they fell for it." For example, the student from Rural Retreat High School said about Blevins, "He told me I was the one person he could always trust. He'd just single me out and make me feel good." She in turn assured him by saying, "If you ever need somebody to talk to, you can talk to me." And Blevins did, manipulating the young woman into a deeper relationship by indicating he needed her to help resolve his suicidal thoughts. It was a relationship that eventually led to sex in his office in the high school wrestling room. Blevins was sentenced in December 1998 to serve twenty-five years in prison.

One reason some adults are drawn to adolescents and younger children, experts in the field say, is that they are so easy to manipulate. "If you try to approach an adult, it can be scary," said Robert Prentky, the director of assessment at the Justice Resource Center in Massachusetts. "It's far less likely that a child is going to reject you." And as W. Richard Fossey, dean of the college of education at Louisiana State University, suggests, predators like Blevins "have an uncanny ability to pick a child who is needy, has poor communication with his or her parents and is a kid who isn't going to tell." Students who lack strong relations with parents and peers or face unusual stress may be more receptive to the attention and more intimidated by threats. Edward Stancik, the special commissioner for the New York City school system, asserts, "It's also because they're less likely to be believed. They're seen as an easy mark and low risk."

Michael Dwayne Blevins fits our profile of the predator teacher. His major goal is to satisfy his sexual desires, not form a helping relationship. As W. Richard Fossey suggests, he had the uncanny ability to pick a child who was needy, had poor communication with her parents, and was a kid who wasn't going to tell. A kid who, as Edward Stancik suggests, was an easy mark and, most important, less likely to be believed if she came forward and asked for help. Our secondary schools are filled with students like this. Some are needy teens at the margins of school life, who have a pattern of continuous failure and acting-out behavior. They are often anonymous and written off as on their way to dropping out. Others are successful students who have troubled home lives and estranged relationships with parents that they keep to themselves, not students you would expect to have troubles and most certainly not be involved in a sexual relationship with a teacher. Both groups are vulnerable to drifting into risky relationships because their need for caring adult contact is so great, relationships that again are often obvious to observing students whose suspicion is aroused by the close contact between the teacher and student but not recognized by the victims involved. They see no warning signs or red light because they want so much to be loved and cared for.

## THE CASE OF RICHARD PLASS

Richard Plass, a renowned teacher and assistant principal at Stuyvesant High School in New York City, was arrested on May 21, 1999, and charged with molesting a fifteen-year-old ninth grade student who had volunteered to work as his assistant. Plass, fifty-five, had worked at Stuyvesant for the past sixteen years and taught in the city system for thirty-three years. The abuse took place in 1998 in Plass's office at the school.[3] During the first encounter he attempted to rub the girl's leg and tried to hug her while he viewed pornographic websites. The girl told investigators that she consistently rebuffed Plass's advances. On other occasions Plass masturbated in the girl's presence and tried to touch her genitals. Investigators learned of the incidents from a teacher who read a journal that the girl was keeping as part of a class. In her entries, which were made in February 1999, the girl wrote about the incidents as if they were happening to a friend.

Plass was no ordinary teacher and Stuyvesant is no ordinary school. Plass, a biology teacher, was best known for encouraging students to enter the competition for the annual Westinghouse science competition, recently renamed Intel Science Talent Research. For sixteen years he pushed students to enter the contest and then shepherded their progress through the entry procedure. In his career at Stuyvesant Plass oversaw

250 finalists and two dozen winners, more winners than any other high school in America. Stuyvesant, one of the elite high schools in New York City, has long been known for producing a number of finalists for the Intel program each year, helping fortify its reputation as one of the finest public schools in the country. Plass was a star teacher in a star school. Bright and ambitious students flocked to Stuyvesant, hoping to gain enrollment in the highly coveted multiyear science program he administered in order to compete in the Intel competition. He and his program were a major drawing card for the best and brightest New York City students. He held the keys to which students entered and which students were rejected, and he could make or break students once they were in the program. In a real sense he was his own boss and seemingly not subject to the rules and boundaries observed by colleagues. He was on his own, enthroned in a position of power in which he sexually abused and harassed students, knowing that if they spoke out he had the power to drop them from the program. The fifteen-year-old abused student had volunteered to help in Plass's office in hopes of entering the Intel program. However, she was only the latest of Plass's victims. Investigators disclosed that other students in the Intel program reported that he had made inappropriate comments to them and looked down girls' shirts in class.[4] The students did not report the incidents because they feared the powerful teacher would kick them out.

Plass's predatory behavior apparently was known to school officials. In fact, Plass was allowed to transfer to Stuyvesant High from Grover Cleveland High School in Queens, New York, after complaints were filed against him for sexually harassing students there, complaints that could no longer be pursued because a three- to five-year statute of limitations in such cases had run out. At Stuyvesant complaints were filed against Plass by female students in 1985 and 1992, complaints that resulted only in a reprimand for Plass. In August 1999 Plass pleaded guilty to sexually harassing the fifteen-year-old student and received three years probation as part of a plea bargain.

There are many obvious lessons in the Plass case. For example,

1. The Plass case serves as a reminder that despite its vaunted academic standing, Stuyvesant was as vulnerable as any other school to such acts.[5]

2. Students enrolled in highly competitive high schools and special programs often fear to speak out against teachers on whom they rely for
entrance into coveted school programs, high grades, and recommendations for college. As student body president David Meadvin suggests,
it is unfair to expect students to openly confront teachers like Plass,
who hold so much power over them.

3. Administrators and colleagues can turn a blind eye to the predatory behaviors of powerful entrepreneur teachers like Plass, who are seen as
deities and drawing cards to enhance the school's reputation and allowed to set their own personal agendas and boundaries. Although
there were complaints against Plass in 1985 and 1992, all he received
was a reprimand. Incredibly, he was applying to be the school's new
principal and was interviewed for the job only days before his arrest in
May 1999. He was in the club and apparently felt beyond reproach and
detection, even qualified to become principal.

4. Students are aware of the behavior of predator teachers like Plass and want
administrators and teachers to act. It simply can't be left up to the students
alone to sound the alarm, particularly with a powerful teacher like Plass.

5. Predator teachers like Plass can avoid detection in large high schools
that lack close teacher–student helping relationships. Stuyvesant is
housed in a ten-story building and has as enrollment of 3,100 students.
It is a school, as reported by Randall C. Archibold, in which students
report that student–teacher relationships are never particularly warm
and where students have the reputation of doing anything they must in
order to stay on the good side of faculty members. Students reported
that Plass was not someone that they felt comfortable going to with
their problems. Most students did not look at him as a friend or someone who could be supportive of their needs.

6. Many predators like Plass leave a trail. For example, like Michael
Blevins, they have moved on from schools where they have been involved in sexual misconduct.

7. Observing and caring teachers can intervene and help abused students
even when a cry for help is disguised as an incident happening to a
friend, as in the case of the fifteen-year-old student abused by Plass.

The Plass case, however, suggests another subtler, less obvious lesson.
When sexual abuse involves a star teacher or coach, as in the case of John

Shockro, it has the potential to damage the reputation of the school, school district, and the star teachers involved. In these situations the victim's cry for help may be less likely to be believed and the needs of the institution for survival take over in an "it can't happen here" response. Stuyvesant senior David Meadvin, eighteen, zeroed in on this lesson when he said to reporter Andrew Jacob, "If the allegations are true they should be dealt with, but I hope this doesn't overshadow all the good things about the school." Meadvin is not talking about the damage to the lives of harassed students. He is talking about the institution and the potential damage to the school's reputation. The need to help the students who are victims of the Plasses and the Shockros and to implement a training, supervision, monitoring, and intervention program to stop such behaviors collide with the self-serving aspects of school life. This self-serving approach argues, "How will this case hurt our reputation as a safe, student-centered learning environment with strong academic programs? How will this case impact on our enrollment and recruiting efforts? Will these incidents of harassment make our school appear less special and innovative?"

Yet as in the case of John Shockro and Richard Plass, there were caring and courageous adults, a policewoman and a teacher, who challenged the self-serving status quo and acted on behalf of the students involved. They refused to allow school leaders to ignore or blame the victim in order to prevent a crack in the school's reputation.

## THE CASE OF JOHN SCHAENMAN

Some cases of alleged sexual misconduct by teachers blur the lines between innocent and some would say naive teachers who go beyond the call of duty to act as mentors, advisers, and coaches for needy students and teachers who use their close relationship with students to lure them into unwanted sexual relationships. The case of John Schaenman raises some of the complicated issues that arise when teachers become involved in such close relationships with students. We have no proof that Schaenman was a predator. In fact, he was found not guilty of charges that he took indecent liberties with a student. However, the case does point out the potential mischief that can occur when a highly regarded teacher sets his own questionable boundaries with students. Here is the story and the issues and implications involved when training, supervision, monitoring, and intervention are absent.

Schaenman was an elementary school teacher in New Hope, North Carolina.[6] He was also a soccer coach who spent time mentoring boys. He invited youngsters to play tennis with him, spend the night at his apartment, and take trips out of town. In 1993 a twenty-year-old man alleged that Schaenman took indecent liberties. While a judge dismissed the charges, the case made a lot of people, both parents and teachers, uncomfortable. Schaenman declined to comment but many of his colleagues said he left himself open to attack by allowing students to spend the night at his apartment. Kaufman reports that Elvia Walker, who has been an educator for twenty-nine years, said teachers could form close relationships with children without raising questions of impropriety. "I've had kids who could tell me anything," said Walker, principal of West Cary Middle School. "It never would have crossed my mind to have them spend the night. There was a line that I didn't cross and a line they didn't cross. If you are mature and old enough to teach, there are some givens." Ann Majestic, the attorney for the Durham and Wake school systems, said she still doesn't recommend that schools dictate the level of appropriate contact because that could discourage any relationships whatsoever. "I advocate no dating, no romantic relationships, but all the community-based programs have the primary purpose of adult males spending time with students away from school." That's where schools face a conflict. They don't want to discourage teachers and volunteers from being role models for children. Trinia Holeman, a colleague of Schaenman at New Hope Elementary, suggests, "It is important for children to see us as friends, human beings and role models. Sometimes in social situations they learn from us not so much about academics but life. As teachers we want to touch the lives of children." Teachers who go beyond what is expected of them in the classroom such as taking students on trips or even into their homes to work on projects are often considered the best.

Schaenman also fits my profile of teachers at risk for sexual misconduct. He blurred the boundaries between his professional and personal life by inviting students to spend the night at his apartment, spent much of his free time mentoring boys, and took them on trips out of town. As his colleagues suggested, he was inviting trouble and leaving himself open to attack. He appeared to ignore or was unable to see the red light of danger as he engaged in these activities. He didn't put in place a line, as Elvia Walker suggests, that "I didn't cross and they didn't cross . . . there are some givens." Schaenman's risky behavior was either ignored by parents, colleagues, and administrators or, as in the case of some parents, praised because they reported that Schaenman was a wonderful influence on their children. But clearly Schaenman operated on his own until being charged with indecent liberties. Schaenman was cleared and returned to teaching.

This case illuminates the problems that can occur when adult male or female teachers, who lack training, supervision, monitoring, and the necessary intervention when sexual misconduct is a possibility, become involved as mentors for students. Educators and parents in the Triangle area of Raleigh, North Carolina, say there is a need to establish boundaries between adults and students outside the classroom, but there is no consensus on where to draw the line. Elvia Walker's response that "if you're mature and old enough to teach, there are some givens," while sounding like welcome advice, isn't enough to help some teachers establish boundaries and avoid sexual misconduct. We are not talking here about age and maturity. Being an adult and mature by community standards does little to prepare teachers for the complicated professional and personal issues that emerge when they are asked to serve as role models, mentors, advisers, personal advocates for students, and so on. Whatever title we bestow on teachers, it is incumbent on us to prepare them for how to handle these roles and encourage them to reach out for help when they find themselves crossing boundaries. Unfortunately age and maturity are of little help when the personal needs of teachers meet the personal needs of students head-on, especially as in the case of Schaenman, where there is no one listening and help isn't on the way until it's too late.

## THE CASE OF KENNETH DELUCA

According to the Ontario (Canada) Province Ministry of Attorney General's report on April 9, 1996, Kenneth DeLuca pleaded guilty to fourteen sexual offenses involving thirteen victims.[7] The crimes took place between 1972 and 1993. Each was committed while DeLuca was a teacher with Sault Ste. Marie Roman Catholic School Board. All of his victims were females; all but one was a student. Their ages ranged from ten to eighteen. The report suggests that DeLuca represents the ultimate breach of the trust placed in a teacher—a teacher who preys on students. However, as we have seen in many of the cases presented in this book, DeLuca's predatory behavior was known early on by administrators, colleagues, and parents. As early as 1973, and at numerous times thereafter, complaints were made about DeLuca's conduct to principals, other teachers, and school board officials. Though the complaints were well founded, they were not acted on. DeLuca's sexual misconduct continued for twenty years as he easily moved from school to school.

As I have documented in this book, the report confirms that DeLuca's case was not unique and follows a pattern similar to other sexual misconduct cases. For example, teachers were reluctant to report suspected sexual misconduct by a colleague, victims and their parents were intimidated to prevent or discourage disclosure, misconduct was not acted on, and the suspected predator was transferred from school to school. As the report states, "The response of the School Board and its employees to complaints or disclosures made by the victims was completely inadequate and, indeed, harmful. It involved, at times, stereotypical notions of what could be expected from a truthful victim, a minimizing of the seriousness of DeLuca's misconduct, a lack of objectivity and a self-serving approach to these complaints."

The report cites a review of the DeLuca case begun in May 1999 by Sydney J. Robins, a former judge of the Court of Appeals for Ontario, which resulted in 101 recommendations for change that specifically address "teacher–student sexual misconduct in the elementary and secondary schools."[8] This review supports five major arguments I make in this book by stating the following:

- "The vast majority of teachers are unquestionably highly dedicated and caring professionals who seek to ensure a safe learning environment."
- "There is no typical offence or offender in sexual misconduct cases. While sexual misconduct by teachers is perpetrated overwhelmingly by males, and overwhelmingly against females, it occurs in all combinations of gender. The popular conception that anyone who sexually abuses a child is a pedophile is simply wrong. In fact, teachers who engage in sexual misconduct with children and adolescents are not pedophiles in most cases. Terms such as 'boundary violators,' 'romantic-

bad judgment abusers' or 'situational offenders' have been used to describe different types of abusers."

- "Students abused by teachers probably delay disclosure by reason of deference to an authority figure, embarrassment, guilt and fear—fear of retaliation by the abuser, fear that no one will believe them, fear of being blamed and fear of some sort of punishment. A child's desire to comply with the request of an adult he or she trusts and by whom he or she wishes to be accepted is another inhibitor of disclosure. The genuine affection a child may have for the teacher, especially one who promotes the 'special relationship' and who has spent a great deal of time in the grooming phase, should not be underestimated."
- "Teachers fear that a heightened sensitivity to potential accusations of sexual misconduct will have a chilling effect on a friendly and nurturing school environment. They are no doubt appalled by conduct such as Kenneth DeLuca's and are understandably concerned that such conduct may unfairly reflect upon them and their profession."
- "It must be concluded that the DeLuca case is neither aberrant or out of date. Teacher sexual misconduct is sufficiently prevalent to warrant special attention. Arguments to the contrary should not be allowed to forestall efforts to understand the problem and actively address it."

Sexual misconduct doesn't just happen. As the case studies in chapters 2–4 suggest, sexual misconduct occurs in an environment in which teachers and coaches are allowed to operate on their own without needed training, supervision, monitoring, and intervention. They are allowed to cross boundaries even when their destructive behavior is observed by administrators, colleagues, students, parents, and community members. These otherwise responsible members of the school community are seemingly frozen into inaction by the behaviors involved in sexual misconduct, as are the victims. It's an "it can't happen here" mentality. They look the other way, don't speak out, and tend to mistrust their own sound judgment, particularly when the misconduct involves a star teacher or coach and students, who as Old Rochester Junior High principal Robert Gardner describes, are erroneously labeled as given to sexual fantasies. There is a process that blames the victim who comes forward and defends the abusing educator until he is pursued and the truth becomes known. As some of these case studies reveal, there are examples of some educators being falsely accused. School district leaders do need to examine every aspect of the cases. But they need to be careful, as in the Shockro case, not to be blindsided by long-held allegiances and, as in the case of Robert Gardner, their own biases.[9]

When sexual misconduct occurs, one of the most damaging aftermaths is the loss of faith and trust in adults in the school by students, parents, and even colleagues. Suspicion takes over. Teachers close their doors. Help for a needy student is harder to find. Rumors abound. In almost every situation—from the cases of Glenn Harris, Gwendolyn Hampton, and Dr. D, Alois Dlhopolsky, to the cases of Richard Plass, John Shockro, and Joseph Daddio and the Southington High School coaches—the school climate in which the misconduct occurred changed dramatically. Students and parents became more wary of teachers who were committed to helping their students resolve personal as well as academic problems. As Southington resident Matthew Welinsky said, "You think you can trust teachers and that the children are safe and then you hear about something like this, going on without anyone noticing."[10] Many teachers increased their professional distance from needy students, avoided helping students with personal problems, and warned colleagues to focus on their academic teaching and leave the helping to the professional counselors. Community-based counselors are brought in from outside agencies to temporarily offer support to students. Administrators become more vigilant. As current Southington Superintendent Harvey Polansky said, "We will continue to ensure a safe environment for our students."[11] In the aftermath trust erodes between students and teachers, parents and teachers, teachers and teachers, and teachers and administrators. The community counselors leave and teachers close their doors to helping needy students. The result? A double whammy. The training, supervision, monitoring, and intervention that might have lowered the possibility of the sexual misconduct is still absent while the school climate becomes marked by suspicion and self-protection. The victims in this scenario are once again the needy, vulnerable students who desperately need a caring adult mentor and teachers who want to help these students.

As we proceed to chapter 5, with its emphasis on training, supervision, helpful peer observations, and intervention to solve the problem of sexual misconduct in the schools, let me summarize what we know about the problem, data that can help us formulate how best to proceed.

1. There is no "epidemic" of teacher sexual misconduct but it is a problem that must be addressed.

2. Pedophiles and psychotics represent only a small percentage of teachers involved in sexual misconduct. They should be weeded out by effective early screening in the hiring and supervision process. The vast majority of teachers and coaches involved in sexual misconduct are otherwise successful professionals who find themselves ill-prepared to handle close contact with needy students. The major emphasis on solving the problem of sexual misconduct should be aimed at this latter group.

3. Training for teachers and coaches should focus on the notion that every teacher can be at risk to sexual misconduct given a clustering together of certain professional and personal circumstances. These may be family problems involving divorce, death, illness, and so on. Some teachers may unwittingly seek emotional connections through close personal involvement with equally needy students. A professional setback may also trigger the need for close involvement that is being denied in the adult world.

4. Teachers who serve as coaches, advisers, mentors, and leaders in extracurricular activities appear to be the most vulnerable to sexual misconduct, particularly if they are very successful, politically connected, and seen as community icons but at the same time lack training in how to engage in close contact with students. If these successful professionals become involved in sexual misconduct, they are often given a pass by administrators, colleagues, parents, and community leaders with whom they hold long-term allegiances and political connections. As a result the failure to confront the problem and the lack of intervention may lead to further misconduct and the adoption of a predatory lifestyle, with the teacher or coaches believing they will not be helped or caught.

5. Teachers and coaches need training, supervision, helpful peer observations and intervention when necessary to avoid sexual misconduct. They need to learn how to carry on close contact with students, many of whom are needy, and how to establish clear boundaries.

6. Each group in the school—administrators, professional helpers such as guidance counselors, teachers, support staff, students, and parents—need training in how they should respond to teachers and coaches who cross professional boundaries.

7. There need to be many open doors for help in the school that the victims of sexual misconduct, their parents, and the professionals involved in the misconduct can walk through for help and intervention that can stop the misconduct early on.

8. Often school districts, teacher unions, and professional associations such as the kind found in athletics are reluctant to offer training to their staff, thinking, "It can't happen here." As a result sexual misconduct by teachers and coaches is treated as an aberration, a bad seed, rather than one of the many problems that can happen to otherwise successful professionals. The result? The problem gets little discussion and little or no training resources. It's a dark topic that is off the agenda. We need to raise awareness about sexual misconduct and take it out of the "no-no" column and place it in the column of "it can happen, particularly without training."

9. Administrators, teachers, support staff, students, parents, and community members are often reluctant to confront teachers and coaches involved in sexual misconduct even when the behavior is obvious and "everyone knows." They fail to trust their judgment and observation skills. They are frozen in denial.

10. The victims of sexual misconduct are often reluctant to come forward and seek intervention. They feel they will not be believed. They fear they will be blamed by their parents and peers and, in the case of gifted academic or athletic students, may be deprived of scholarships and select college admission by mentors who are carrying out the sexual misconduct. They become frozen, unable to confront the problem and ask for help.

11. Teachers and coaches involved in sexual misconduct often fail to come forward and ask for intervention. They feel they will be judged and treated as predators by the school and community. They too remain frozen and without help.

12. Homosexual and lesbian relationships between teachers and students appear to be underreported and in general not given a place in the training programs for teachers and coaches.

13. When sexual misconduct does occur, what often follows is a tendency by teachers to pull back from offering help to needy students, close their doors, which results in a school climate of suspi-

cion and rumors rather than offering the needed training for every teacher in how to carry on close contact with students and set clear boundaries. It is a classic case of problem creation in the guise of problem solution.

14. Outside-of-school activities, such as specialized workshops, camps, tournaments, and classes for gifted academic and athletic students need to be monitored by school leaders in order to help their students avoid coaches and teachers who are at risk for sexual misconduct.

## NOTES

1. William Swiggart, Karen Starr, Reid Finlayson, and Anderson Spickard, "Sexual Boundaries and Physicians: Overview and Educational Approach to the Problem," Vanderbilt University Center for Professional Health, 2001, http://mc.vanderbilt.edu/root/vumc/php?site=cph&doc=742 (accessed 13 August 2004).

2. Caroline Hendrie, "In Youth's Tender Emotions Abusers Find Easy Pickings," *Education Week*, 2 December 1998, http://edweek.org/ew/vol-18/14tactic.h18 (accessed 13 August 2004).

3. Andrew Jacobs, "School Official Charged with Molesting Students," *New York Times*, 22 May 1999, 3 (B).

4. David Rhode, "Probation for Teacher Guilty of Abuse at Stuyvesant," *New York Times*, 19 August 1999, 1 (B).

5. Randall C. Archibold, "A Chill at Stuyvesant High," *New York Times*, 21 September 1999, 1, 8 (B).

6. Susan Kaufman, "When Teachers Mix Socially with Students," *News & Observer*, 29 September 1994, 1, 12 (A).

7. Ontario Province Ministry of the Attorney General, "Chapter 1: The Nature and Scope of the Review," Review of Kenneth DeLuca Case, 1999, http://www.attorneygeneral.jus.gov.on.ca/english/about/pubs/robins/ch1.asp (accessed 26 February 2005).

8. Ontario Province Ministry of the Attorney General, "Chapter III: Extent and Nature of Teacher-Student Sexual Misconduct," Review of Kenneth DeLuca case, 1999, http://attorneygeneral.jus.gov.on.ca/English/about/pubs/robins/ch3.asp (accessed 26 February 2005).

9. Michael Levinson, "Ex-principal Rejects Naming Honor," boston.com, 12 December 2004, http://boston.com/news/local/articles/2004/12/ex_principal_rejects_naming_hon (accessed 12 December 2004).

10. *Southington Journal*, "Town's Disgust Outlasts a Statute of Limitations," *New York Times*, 14 January 2002, 17 (A).

11. Kimberly W. Moy and William Schubert, "Coaches Avoid Charges in Sex Allegations," *Hartford Courant*, 10 January 2002, 7 (A1).

## Chapter Five

# Training Teachers, Coaches, and Students to Avoid Sexual Misconduct

This "how-to" chapter is designed to prepare building administrators to implement a training program so they and their staff are ready and set to deal with the complex issues involved in sexual misconduct. This training can best be utilized as part of a broad staff development effort to prepare teachers for roles as personal adult advocates, advisers, mentors, coaches, and club leaders, roles that bring teachers, coaches, and students together in close, long-term contact. This final chapter fills a gap in the effort to prepare building administrators to deal with sexual misconduct. For example, administrators have been warned about the legal aspects of sexual misconduct, liabilities, and lawsuits, and they have been given information, handouts, and manuals warning teachers, students, and parents about would-be predators. As researcher Elaine Yaffe points out in her article "Expensive, Illegal, and Wrong: Sexual Harassment in Our Schools," there is no shortage of published and filmed material designed to help students, teachers, and other staff members become better equipped to deal with these changing times.[1] There are prepared curricula and handbooks containing a wealth of information and definitions of what sexual harassment is, background and summaries of relevant laws, sample policies, instructions on how to conduct an investigation, lesson plans, overheads, first-person accounts of actual incidents, newspaper clippings, quizzes to uncover preconceptions and misinformation, and videos that attempt to give the sense and feel of the problem.

I argue that while we have given administrators the helpful information that Yaffe suggests, we have failed to provide administrators with a road map on how to train their teachers to deal with close contact with students that can spawn sexual misconduct. The absence of an easily implemented training program has left a glaring gap in our efforts to raise the awareness and competency of administrators when it comes to sexual misconduct preparedness. We have failed to deliver what administrators needed in every case study in this book: training, supervision, and intervention. The result? We have left teachers, coaches, and students at risk for sexual misconduct, as well as the administrators.

As Frederick N. Brown, associate executive director of the National Association of Elementary School Principals, suggests, turning a blind eye to sexual misconduct is "a career-ending move for a principal. If it's found that you covered up or overlooked something that harmed a child, you might as well pack it in."[2] As mentioned in chapter 3, Old Rochester principal Robert Gardner's seeming protection of John Shockro entailed huge personal and professional costs.[3] He too was Shockro's victim in that he endured the scorn of many community members and was forced to request the removal of a plaque dedicated to his service to the school and the community. Principal Gardner provides an unfortunate example of what can happen to otherwise caring and competent administrators when sexual misconduct training is not available. Perhaps if Gardner had the training program I present in this chapter, John Shockro might have been helped before he caused harm to vulnerable teens and ruined his own personal and professional life.

Writer Caroline Hendrie suggests that a lack of training leaves many well-intentioned administrators with little understanding of the dynamics of staff-on-student sexual abuse. But her helpful words can never convey the pain and hurt that can come to administrators, teachers, coaches, and student victims when there exists a "lack of training" in our secondary schools.

We need to sell school and community leaders on why it is better to prepare teachers and coaches for the hazards and risks involved in close contact with students rather than leave them at risk and vulnerable to sexual misconduct. In the absence of training and intervention we should not be surprised when sexual misconduct occurs. The combination of untrained teachers in close contact with needy students is an accident waiting to happen, an accident that comes with great costs to the individuals involved, the school district, and the community. As with other successful reform efforts, our first step is to build a support base and make it attractive for teachers and administrators to buy into such training, to see such training as being in their own self-interest, important to their personal and professional development, and having the potential to make them more effective teachers.

In the next section I focus on the specific steps needed to train teachers by beginning with an overview of the issues involved in sexual misconduct. I then present my three-part Teacher Sexual Misconduct Awareness Inventory (TSMAI), which administrators can use in concert with the training resources of pupil personnel workers such as guidance counselors, athletic directors, teacher leaders, and community mental health resources to raise teachers' awareness about the potential problems involved in close contact with students and how to set boundaries. However, no training program is foolproof. Clearly marked open doors for intervention need to be put in place to guide teachers and students headed toward sexual misconduct. In the final section I focus on how administrators, counselors, social workers, school psychologists, students, support staff, parents, and community members on the front lines of the school can observe teachers unwittingly heading into friendship, love, or sexual relationships with students. Each group will be able to channel observations to administrators who are prepared to provide quick intervention to stop the relationship and direct the teacher and students involved to credible sources of help in the school and community. This section also highlights the important part of listening to "chatter" among students in the hallways, lunchroom, athletic events, and dances and to concerned colleagues and parents. Members of the school community often know when relationships between teachers and students become special and teachers take on risky behaviors, such as taking a student to lunch, giving her a ride home, selecting her as an athletic assistant, buying gifts, and taking on the role of savior, parent surrogate, friend, or lover.

## SELLING THE PROFESSIONAL STAFF, PARENTS, AND COMMUNITY MEMBERS ON THE VALUE OF TRAINING TO AVOID SEXUAL MISCONDUCT

As I have suggested, training teachers to understand the hazards and risks involved in close, long-term relationships with needy and vulnerable students is rarely handled in a proactive way by school administrators, teacher union leaders, and parent/community activists. Rather, it is either considered a taboo subject, one that "can't happen here," or approached solely by giving the professional staff information on the legal aspects of sexual misconduct and implementing a screening process to rid the school of sexual predators.

Screening out predators becomes the focus rather than acknowledging that every teacher, given the right conditions, can be at risk for misconduct. This is a shortsighted remedy at best and, rather than solving the problem, leaves the professional staff vulnerable to sexual misconduct. It is problem creating under the guise of problem solving. The result? Teachers, teacher-advisers, coaches, mentors, and leaders of extracurricular clubs remain at risk to sexual misconduct as they continue to engage students in a variety of helping and supporting roles that are being called for by secondary school reform efforts, such as *Turning Points 2000: Educating Adolescents in the 21st Century*[4] and *Breaking Ranks II: Strategies for Leading High School Reform.*[5]

How do we turn the conversation around and raise the awareness of educators, parents, and community leaders? Before any discussion of training, we need to mount a selling campaign to put the issue of sexual misconduct on the school's agenda. I propose that the best approach is to suggest, "Isn't it better, and in the long run more cost effective, to train teachers about the hazards and risks of close contact with students, how to set boundaries, and to recognize the signs of potential misconduct within themselves and their colleagues rather than leave them on their own without the necessary training and skills they need?" Part of this selling process should emphasize that teachers need a variety of skills to do their work well. And these skills need to cover a variety of different areas that include students' academic and personal development. We need to ask why school districts provide staff development on issues such as discipline, bullying, inclusion, equity, and so on, and leave out training teachers for close contact with students. We can't simply tell teachers to assume a role of advocate, adviser, or mentor with students without providing the necessary training and skill acquisition. That is a recipe for failure, failure on the part of some teachers because they are unprepared for this new role and naively set out in this new role to become saviors, parent surrogates, friends, and, for some, lovers. They are allowed to drift down a path of personal destruction for both teacher and needy teenager. In the selling process we need to remind school and community leaders that even if the training and intervention helps only one teacher or coach to avoid the path to sexual misconduct, this kind of proactive intervention can save an otherwise successful professional, his or her family, the student involved, and his or her parents from public humiliation and hurt.

We need to remind school and community leaders that there are other costs than the personal one for the teacher, student, and parents directly involved. There are the economic costs. Training may save the district from paying out large sums to victims of sexual misconduct. There is the cost of the loss of trust in the school district and staff, and the damage to a positive school climate that often occurs in the aftermath of a case of sexual misconduct. What often follows is an atmosphere of fear, which includes rumors of alleged misconduct, finger pointing, and teachers closing their doors to close contact with needy students, feeling that they too could become at risk to false allegations. There is also the cost of community discontent with the district and district leaders, which often results in voting down school budgets and firing administrators. The message in our sales campaign needs to be clear: As leaders in the school district and community you have a lot to gain by acting and also a lot to lose by not acting. We need to do whatever it takes to avoid putting our professional staff and students in harm's way and avoid destroying the image that the school district is a safe and nurturing place.

The growing need for reforming our secondary schools, as suggested in the *Breaking Ranks II* report, may be just the vehicle needed to help persuade school and community leaders to address the prevention of sexual misconduct. For example, the *Breaking Ranks II* report calls for each student to have a personal adult advocate to help him or her personalize the educational experience, a professional staff member who knows the aspirations, strengths, and weakness of each student and helps him or her become successful in all classes and activities. The report also recommends that teachers (1) convey a sense of caring to their students so they feel their teachers have a stake in their learning and (2) become adept coaches and facilitators to promote active involvement of students in their own learning. Requiring teachers to move from a strictly academic focus into the role of personal adult advocate who knows each student well demonstrates a high degree of caring and facilitates the active involvement of each student's needs to include training on how to carry on close contact with students. That means helping teachers move from a lecture-based style of communicating and interacting with students into a facilitating style in which students talk to their teacher/personal advocate about personal, health, and well-being issues that may be impacting negatively on their academic success. For teachers that means learning how to listen, be nonjudgmental, advise, intervene, and help students resolve problems and, as *Breaking Ranks II* suggests, interact with "hard to reach" parents through home visits, Saturday meetings, and meetings outside regular business hours.

Training will be required to bring teachers into the personal adult advocate role model that emphasizes much more close, long-term personal contact with students. That training will require attention to the hazards and risks involved in such close contact, developing skills on how to set boundaries with needy students, avoiding becoming a savior, parent surrogate, friend, or lover with a student, and how to seek intervention when signs of a growing personal relationship with a student begin to evolve. In this way the issue of sexual misconduct can be addressed quietly as part of a broader staff development effort to ready teachers for more student-centered roles, such as a personal adult advocate, adviser, mentor, coach, or club leader. In a sense this approach provides a way for teachers to talk about the issue of sexual misconduct as part of a broader conversation about what takes place when teachers take on new and untried roles, that there are risks and hazards involved, that it can happen but there are ways to prevent it from happening. In a sense this is a win-win situation. Not only do we prepare teachers for the roles that will be required in secondary schools in the future but we also head off future cases of sexual misconduct by connecting this issue to the skills they will need in the future. This approach also moves the discussion of sexual misconduct into the realm of a potential problem for every teacher and away from the argument that it is only a problem for predator teachers. I believe this approach goes a long way toward helping teachers not to be frozen into inaction when they see colleagues, or themselves, moving beyond acceptable teacher–student boundaries.

Placing the issue of sexual misconduct into a broader training program has the advantage of removing some of the notoriety and mystique surrounding the topic and reducing anxiety for teachers. This is a far better approach than training that focuses solely on teachers who become involved in sexual misconduct as mainly predators and pedophiles. Shakeshaft reports that 9.6 percent of students in public schools, some 4.5 million pupils, are likely targets of unwanted sexual attention by a teacher or coach during their school years, suggesting that the scope of the problem appears to far exceed the priest abuse scandal in the Catholic Church.[6]

I believe training that begins with an approach like this, which suggests there is an epidemic of teacher sexual misconduct that is not unlike the Catholic Church crisis, is doomed from the start. Not only is it anxiety producing for the teachers and administrators involved but also for students, parents, and community members. Simply put, teachers, like all learners, don't respond to teaching and training that makes them anxious, defensive, unsure, and vulnerable to an anxious student body, parents, and community. As Michael Pons, a spokesman for the National Education Association (NEA) suggests in his reaction to the Shakeshaft report, *Educator Sexual Misconduct: A Synthesis of Existing Literature,*[7] most people, especially parents, will not read the report and understand its nuances. Instead they will hear "one in ten children is abused in school." Alarming students, parents, and staff with statistics, questionable or not, doesn't solve the problem of sexual misconduct but instead creates other more insidious problems for caring professionals.[8] I believe using numbers, horror stories of predators, and, as the educator sexual misconduct report suggests, creating a coordinator position in each school district to whom "all rumors or allegations or complaints should be channeled" will simply drive caring educators into a self-protection mode with the goal of remaining out of the sight and reach of the case coordinator. The result? Teachers will be more apt to be frozen into inaction rather than becoming a source of intervention, help, and support when they observe a colleague drifting into close relationships with students. It encourages a "not my responsibility or problem" response by teachers. Doors are closed, teachers become wary of close contact, and they decline to be club leaders, advisers, or chaperones.

Therefore, I believe the key to effective training for how teachers and coaches can successfully handle close contact with students and create necessary boundaries lies in giving them the skills required for such relationships. This approach avoids the message that there is an epidemic of sexual misconduct, which often raises anxiety among teachers and coaches and reduces close contact with students. Our work needs to be about removing the mystique surrounding the issue of sexual misconduct, taking it out of the closet, and persuading and training educators that they can prepare themselves to handle this problem just as they learn to handle other student–teacher problems. In a sense our training needs to help teachers and coaches develop a protective barrier between themselves and needy students. Not a barrier that prevents caring, helping, supporting, guiding, and sharing hard truths. Rather, a barrier that can turn away unwanted (or in some cases wanted) friendship and love overtures from needy students looking for a caring adult role model in their lives. And barriers set off an alarm when teachers and coaches find themselves needy for emotional contact and turn to their students for such connections. Clearly educators require ongoing training, skill development, supervision, support from their colleagues, and timely intervention to help them navigate successfully through myriad problems they encounter at different developmental stages in their ever-changing professional careers and personal lives. I argue that avoiding sexual misconduct needs to be given top priority in our ongoing efforts to ready our teachers and coaches for the risks involved in their work.

In the end this kind of selling campaign to offer teachers and coaches the training they need is directed at challenging some long-held assumptions in our secondary schools, for example:

- Sexual misconduct doesn't happen to teachers who really care about kids. It only happens with sick people.
- Teachers don't need to be their brothers' keepers. They are not paid to monitor colleagues' behavior. It is not up to them to act when they see a colleague crossing boundaries. I don't see any of this taking-care-of-each-other nonsense in our contract.
- The business of school is teaching students to read, write, do math, and so on. Teachers shouldn't be involved as advisers or mentors or be in close contact with students. That's the job of counselors, social workers, school psychologists, and so on.
- Teachers are already too busy dealing with things like testing mandates and standards. They don't have time for training in how to be involved in more personal ways with students.
- Sexual misconduct can't happen here. We have some of the most qualified and dedicated teachers in the country. They wouldn't be foolish enough to become sexually involved with a student.

## TRAINING TEACHERS AND COACHES
## TO AVOID SEXUAL MISCONDUCT

After selling teachers and coaches on the need for training and getting them onboard the process, the next step is to provide them with an overview of the subtle issues involved in how to avoid sexual misconduct. Creating awareness, as is the case in many efforts of educational reform, is the first and necessary step in the effort. As I have suggested, the best approach to this training may be to include it as part of a broader topic, such as training teachers how to be advisers and personal adult advocates and for coaches, the special issues involved in coaching female and male athletes. This training model can also be used to train teachers, coaches, and religious personnel in community and religious education and athletic programs. The training can also be utilized to answer the growing need for training priests, ministers, and rabbis on how to handle close contact with their congregation members, including needy children and teenagers. Here is an example of an overview that can be presented in the opening sessions of training to help create teacher awareness about sexual misconduct, to make it real and believable for them.

## AN OVERVIEW OF THE ISSUES INVOLVED
## IN AVOIDING SEXUAL MISCONDUCT

- The approach I favor in introducing the training is that it is okay to talk about sexual misconduct. It can happen to any professional in our school district. We are all at risk. Therefore we need to be prepared and know how to respond to such risky behavior if we find ourselves or our colleagues crossing professional boundaries and becoming too involved with students, as saviors, friends, surrogate parents, or potential lovers. Everyone can benefit from this training. The key is to create a dialogue among educators that moves the issue of sexual misconduct from the denial stage to reality.
- Acknowledge that transference of affection between students and teachers is common in many classrooms and is an important part of the learning process. Students who are cared for and whose contributions are valued tend to be better learners. They are more involved and less likely

to offer resistance. These students begin to feel toward the teacher as they have felt toward other important people in their lives and expect the teacher to deal with them as those important people have or should have done. Teachers who are valued by their students and deemed worthy also tend to be more effective. They are more involved and more apt to risk close contact with their students. For example, in a caring classroom environment the personal lives and stories of students become known through daily teacher–student conversations, which encourage close contact. Teachers get to know about their students' parents, siblings, peers, home life, economic status, dreams, hopes, and failures in passing conversations. And in these conversations the personal lives of teachers also become known to their students, for example, the teacher's marital status, children, home life, outside of school activities, hopes, dreams, and failures. There is a common bond established which suggests that knowing more about our lives will help us establish a classroom learning environment that will enable us to be better students and teachers. But these kinds of intimate classroom conditions can plant the seeds for sexual misconduct if teachers are not skilled enough to erect clear boundaries and avoid becoming saviors, friends, parent surrogates, and even lovers with their students.

• Transference of affection between teachers and students can have a downside when the teacher's own needs for emotional and physical contact are not being met outside the school environment. While transference is a powerful issue in the teacher–student learning process, it is seldom discussed and is not fully understood by administrators and teachers. For example, teachers who are in great need of close emotional and physical contact in their personal lives are at great risk when they become involved in close relationships with students. These may be needs that may have suddenly emerged due to a personal loss such as the death or serious illness of loved one, needs that may be satisfied by becoming increasingly involved in close contact with students who are themselves needy. These teachers may find themselves naively crossing boundaries and, as the saying goes, looking for love in all the wrong places. These can be very successful teachers who become overwhelmed by life's problems and turn to using their close contact with students to meet their personal need for belonging.

• Transference of affection to favorite students who are more like us can have its downside. Simply put, liking certain students too much can put one's professional career in peril. We all come into the education profession carrying assets and liabilities from our own backgrounds. Each of us tends to seek out certain types of students, students we are attracted to, feel safe with, and enjoy helping and communicating with. These are the students who may be fun to be around, seek out our help and advice, honor and respect us for our seeming wisdom, and light up when we walk into a room. These are the students who are given home or cell phone numbers and e-mail addresses by some teachers who enjoy their close, seemingly special relationship. These kinds of "special" teacher–student relationships are found in every middle school, junior high, and high school. Look around your school. These kinds of relationships are not hard to find. But they are also red lights that signal possible trouble ahead. Be careful. Proceed with caution.

• Transference of affection between teachers and students that focuses on saving the student from personal problems, such as an abusive home life, can trigger involvement in sexual misconduct. Again, each of us comes into the classroom having survived many of life's problems. We've gone down some tough roads. Maybe our parents were divorced, we've lost a parent to an early death, we've been abandoned, or we've grown up in an alcohol- or drug-addicted family environment. We managed to make it out of that risky family environment, often with the help of a caring teacher, and become successful teachers ourselves. Yet we still remember what it was like being a teenager in that rocky home environment, and when we come in close contact with students dealing with the same problems, we want to help. We want to help them move on to a better world as our teachers helped us. Therefore, because of our own personal experiences as teenagers, we tend to want to help students with certain problems that we too have experienced. But in the process of helping, sometimes our good intentions get lost in the complexities and pain in our students' lives. We don't see the barriers, the boundaries, and the warning signals. While we do what we can to ease the emotional pain they are going through, it's never enough. Often the problems our students are experiencing, like ours as a child or teenager, don't go away, don't get better, and in fact get worse. We ignore the signals of danger ahead and slide into the role of parent surrogate, thinking we alone can alter this child's life quickly. We may ignore our best judgment that our role is to do all we can to help this child but we are not the parents and we can't take this child home at night, even though the emotion we feel says otherwise. Sexual misconduct can have its beginnings in good intentions, with teachers who because of their own problems as children and teenagers try to save their students from the pain and rough road they traveled. In a sense they move in with the child and become the parent. No, not in the literal sense, but they loan the students money, buy them clothes, remember their birthdays and special holidays, show up at their games, check with other teachers on the students' progress, and seek out needed support such as tutors when needed. And sometimes these relationships naturally flow into love relationships, with the teacher looking to save a needy student and the student looking to be saved, valued, cared for, and thought worthy. Mischief arises out of good intentions that began with the teacher's own struggles as a child and teenager.

- Barriers and signals save lives, whether a steel fence with a warning sign on a winding mountain road or a lighthouse foghorn signaling a treacherous channel ahead. They let us know there is danger ahead and we had best prepare ourselves, be wide awake, vigilant, and responsive. Teachers need barriers and signals when they become involved in close contact with students, barriers that serve as boundaries when they begin heading down a risky road and quickly signal a flashing red light of danger, issuing a jolt that reminds teachers that they have moved into dangerous territory and they had best clear their heads, be vigilant, responsive, and retreat, seeking the counsel of trusted colleagues, administrators, and family members.

The goal of this overview is to point out to teachers that some of the successful practices we employ in the classroom to promote our students' learning and well-being can trigger sexual misconduct if we fail to establish barriers and hear the signal that we are entering a personal relationship that is dangerous. Yes, it is important that we work to create a classroom environment that fosters close relationships between teachers and students. But at the same time we need to tell teachers that it is important to satisfy their own personal needs for affection outside the school environment and to be aware when they begin to seek out students to meet their emotional and physical needs for contact. Teachers need to be reminded that the process of selecting certain students as favorites and awarding them special treatment, a process that in my experience is seen as a normal and okay practice in many schools, is actually risky business. It is also risky business for teachers to take on the role of savior and parent surrogate to try to save their students from life's blows, which the teacher may have received as a child or teenager. I am not saying we should not help needy students. Far from it. Rather, our helping needs to be focused on being an advocate and harnessing every school and community resource we can to help students move on from their troubled lives.

Sexual misconduct, therefore, can result from our good intentions to understand and help our students, trying to meet our own personal need for affection and contact through our students, focusing on students we like and are comfortable with, and taking on the roles of savior and parent rather than teacher and helper. In the end barriers and signals keep teachers stable and focused as they daily negotiate with themselves on how to avoid being a friend, savior, parent, or even lover with their students. Barriers and signals then are the friends of teachers. They remind us that we are human and that our caring can wander off to dangerous places.

But as trainers we need to keep in mind that while this overview may be a valuable first step in helping teachers understand that some of their behavior may trigger sexual misconduct, it probably doesn't lessen their assumption that "it can't happen here." Therefore the next step in the training is to personalize the issue by completing my TSMAI. This inventory can further involve teachers by asking them to reflect on specific questions related to teacher behaviors introduced in the overview.

## PREPARING TEACHERS TO COMPLETE THE TEACHER SEXUAL MISCONDUCT AWARENESS INVENTORY

The next step in readying teachers to avoid sexual misconduct is to have them complete my Teacher Sexual Misconduct Awareness Inventory (TSMAI). In my experience in leading sexual misconduct training programs, an effective way to begin this phase of the training is to show the films *Mr. Holland's Opus*[9] and *Carried Away*[10] and then proceed to the TSMAI.

Both films bring a sense of reality to the training and explore how the personal needs of teachers and students can become entangled in potential or real love affairs.

Teachers in training understand and relate to Mr. Holland. He is a creative teacher with a special gift for caring and involving resistant students. Holland doesn't give up on his students. Rather, he makes himself available and confronts students who are choosing to be passive and not involved. He is a fast learner and is ready to throw out techniques that are failing and risk other approaches. And clearly he is no predator. But early in his fledgling career Holland encounters a different kind of problem student, showing how vulnerable we are as teachers when we enter close relationships with needy students. Holland's problem is not with disciplining acting-out or resistant students. Nor is it a problem that he understands, let alone knows how to solve. Nothing in his graduate teacher education program has prepared him for this event.

The problem is his encounter with Rowena, the female star in the yearly musical he is directing. She is demanding of his attention, always seeming to need more from him—time, praise, private lessons. She says she has family problems. Yet she is a gifted singer and he wants to help her. She sings "I Need Someone To Watch Over Me," and her delivery strongly suggests that "somebody" is Holland. He is flattered by her attention. He is having family problems as well with his wife and deaf son. A part of him wants a new beginning. His star student says, "Come to New York with me," and a part of him wants to go. But somehow he pulls back. He has the skills to sense trouble for himself and for her. He meets her at the bus stop and says, "I can't go." A close call. Tough work on Holland's part. He gives us a look into the struggle and the skills needed not to cross boundaries when a part of us says, "Just this once." Holland's skills? While at first he does not recognize the danger ahead, he slowly awakens to the risks involved, to the fact that his gifted student wants more and more from him. She wants him to leave his teaching job and his family and be with her in faraway, exciting New York City. He fights off the urge to go and slowly comes to terms with the fact that he has some fence mending to do with his wife and son. His wife senses what is happening. She knows he has been spending more and more time after school with Rowena. She's no fool. Her intuition tells her that Holland is halfway out the door. In her own way she confronts him and asks him to work with her to save their marriage. He has a built-in barrier and signal that tells him to be careful, there is thin ice ahead. In spite of his personal troubles he knows that he has a family life and teaching job worth preserving. An important question for teachers, once they have viewed *Mr. Holland's Opus*, is, What would you do if an extremely attractive student sought you out as an adult role model, mentor, or even a father figure or lover?

In *Carried Away* teacher Joseph Svenden is more vulnerable than Holland and lacks some of his skills to resist temptation. He is no predator. He is a man who thinks slowly and deliberately, but his careful approach is not up to the challenge of resisting a precocious seventeen-year-old student who pursues him. At first he balks at the affair but eventually succumbs. The affair may be the first reckless impulse he has ever given in to. Yes, he may have see the alarm of danger ahead. But he is too needy for the physical and emotional contact he lacks in his personal life to take a different course. Svenden is swept away. Important questions for teachers after they have viewed *Carried Away* are, Do you think teachers' needs change over their career lifetime? Are teachers more vulnerable to risk crossing boundaries at certain junctures in their careers? For example, once they receive tenure, are they experiencing midlife crisis in which their personal lives are out of whack, their teaching jobs become less challenging, or are they nearing retirement and facing the anxieties that come with saying good-bye? Have you ever found yourself looking to students for affection, contact, and support when these events occur in your professional or personal life?

Reviewing both these films serves to move the discussion of sexual misconduct from an abstract concept into the reality of what can happen to dedicated and caring teachers when they develop close relationships with students. Completing the TSMAI is the next step in raising teachers' awareness.

## THE TEACHER SEXUAL MISCONDUCT
## AWARENESS INVENTORY: PART 1

This inventory will help raise your awareness about the issue of sexual misconduct. Your answers and observations are important, as they will provide material for our discussions. Please try to answer each question.

1. As teachers we are all attracted to certain students. For example, these may be students you feel a special closeness to and want to spend more time with. We all have our "favorite" students. Please describe these students and what makes them special in your eyes.
2. Effective teacher–student relationships go two ways. Teachers as well as students receive something of value from such relationships. What are you getting in return from students to whom you feel close and consider special?
3. When you were a teenager was there a teacher whom you felt close to, who made you feel special and whom you wanted to spend more time with? Please describe this relationship and any others you have experienced.
4. Are you attracted to helping students with certain kinds of problems? This might be a student affected by a troubled home life, a divorce or separation, a death or serious illness, alcohol and drug addiction, violence, school failure, poor peer relationships, eating disorders, potential suicide, physical, emotional, or sexual abuse, and so on. Please describe these students and your feelings toward them.
5. When you were a teenager, did you experience any of these problems in your life? Briefly describe these problems and their impact on you teaching style now.
6. Do you ever consider taking "problem" students home so they can have a better life, be safe, and be cared for? Have you taken on the role of a parent surrogate by advocating for these students with other teachers, remembering their birthdays, checking on their lives outside of school, even meeting them after school for conferences?
7. Have there been occasions when you had to draw a clear line, a boundary, between yourself and students who wanted too close a relationship, such as a friend, savior, or surrogate parent? Please describe these situations and what made you sense you might be about to cross a professional boundary.
8. How did you distance yourself from these students? Did you remain in their lives as a caring teacher and adviser by setting some kind of workable boundary? Or did you find yourself ignoring the students' advances completely?
9. Did you ever talk, or want to talk, to a colleague, supervisor, friend, or family member about how to avoid becoming too involved in a stu-

dent's personal life and problems while at the same time being an effective adviser and mentor? Please describe your feelings.

10. When you observe a fellow teacher becoming too involved with a student, what is your reaction? Do you approach this teacher and share your concern that he or she may be crossing a professional boundary? Or do you consider it none of your business? Please describe your reaction when you observe a teacher beginning to cross professional boundaries and becoming a friend, savior, or surrogate parent with a student.

12. In most cases of sexual misconduct colleagues and administrators tend to look the other way when they observe a teacher becoming too involved with a student. Unfortunately this leaves the teacher and student involved on their own and sometimes results in a love relationship that leaves both parties scarred for life. Why do you think colleagues and administrators are hesitant to confront such behavior and direct the teacher and student involved to sources of help before it is too late?

13. What are your feelings about teachers who cross professional boundaries and become too involved with their students?

14. Do you think sexual misconduct happens only with male teachers and female students? Do you think female teachers can become involved with male students or that there are homosexual and lesbian relationships that are often underreported?

15. Can you imagine a situation when you might become involved in crossing professional boundaries with a student? After all, you are human and have needs for affection. Sometimes our professional guard does come down. Describe a possible scenario in which you might unwittingly become involved because of your good intentions to help a student.

16. Whom would you turn to for help and advice if you found yourself heading for a friendship, savior, or parent surrogate role with a student?

17. Conversely, how would you respond, what would you say, if a colleague came to you asking for help and advice on how to separate him or herself from a deepening personal relationship with a student?

18. How would you describe "effective professional boundaries" that allow you to become involved in close relationships with students but

at the same time offer a barrier, a layer of protection, from becoming too involved?

## THE TEACHER SEXUAL MISCONDUCT
## AWARENESS INVENTORY: PART 2

In this second section of the TSMAI you will be asked to complete three checklists. These checklists will help you develop a greater in-depth awareness about the issues involved in sexual misconduct, such as the student problems that attract our attention, common hazards and risks for teachers involved in close contact with students, and self controls that help us erect workable boundaries.

Check the student groups and problems you tend to get too involved with:

_____ gifted and talented students
_____ student athletes
_____ male students
_____ female students
_____ gay and lesbian students
_____ students with handicaps
_____ average students
_____ special education students
_____ college-bound students
_____ minority students
_____ acting-out students
_____ students who abuse alcohol
_____ students who abuse drugs
_____ students who abuse tobacco
_____ students returning from rehab
_____ students whose parents are separated or divorced
_____ students who have experienced the death or serious illness of a
         family member or friend
_____ students who are school failures and potential dropouts
_____ students who have an eating disorder such as anorexia or bulimia
_____ students who have suicidal thought or have made suicide attempts

_____ students who have experienced physical, emotional, or sexual abuse

_____ students with poor peer relationships

_____ students with troubled home relationships

Please check the items that you feel represent hazards and risks for teachers involved in close relationships with students:

_____ The teacher holds more than one meeting a week with a certain student. Other students complain that their meeting time is being cut back.

_____ The teacher switches meetings with the student to late afternoon or evening.

_____ The teacher begins to hold meetings at a local diner or in the student's home.

_____ The teacher is flattered by the student's interest in his or her personal life.

_____ The teacher buys the student presents for birthdays and special events.

_____ The teacher writes the student letters of encouragement on a regular basis.

_____ The teacher accompanies the student on field trips.

_____ The teacher drives the student back and forth to school.

_____ The teacher spends time with the student at dances and school activities.

_____ The teacher requests that the student be in his class or homeroom.

_____ The student's parents become concerned about the teacher's overinvolvement with their child.

_____ The student's other teachers and administrators begin to ask questions about the teacher's overinvolvement with the student.

Teachers can avoid the hazards and risks involved in helping by controlling the where, when, and how of the helping process. Here is a checklist of "don'ts." Please check any item that might present a hazard for you.

_____ Don't drive students to school or home alone.

_____ Don't take a student out to breakfast, lunch, or dinner.

_____ Don't buy a student gifts for birthdays or other special occasions.

_____ Don't limit your social life to students and school activities.

_____ Don't limit your need for an ego boost and flattery to students.

_____ Don't shortchange some students by depriving them of an equal amount of meeting time.

_____ Don't write personal letters to students on a regular basis.

_____ Don't hold helping meetings outside of school.

_____ Don't hold helping meetings in the late afternoon or evening.

_____ Don't mix your helping role with your other roles (homeroom teacher, classroom teacher, chaperone, field trip organizer).

_____ Don't neglect to communicate with parents, colleagues, and administrators.

## THE TEACHER SEXUAL MISCONDUCT AWARENESS INVENTORY: PART 3

Part 3 of the TSMAI provides examples of how teacher advisers can talk to students about clear boundaries and how teachers and administrators can intervene and help colleagues who are ignoring the hazards and risks involved with students who are asking for friendship, savior, surrogate parent, and even love relationships. The focus of this last part of the TSMAI is to help teachers and administrators consider interventional and confrontational practices and conversations that can address potential sexual misconduct behaviors. As these examples demonstrate, timely and direct intervention conversations can serve to help teachers define their adviser role with students and spell out the limits of what help they can offer. Timely and direct conversations by teachers and administrators can open a door of help to colleagues crossing boundaries and "teach" them how to respond to overtures by needy students. The kind of intervention conversations I describe not only protect teachers' professional roles but also present an opportunity for teacher advisers to serve as a model for "teaching" needy students how to set boundaries themselves as they navigate through teen problems with help from many different adult mentors. Interacting with a teacher or coach who clearly states, "I can offer you support, but I can't be your friend or parent," can bring a heavy dose of reality and awareness to needy students seeking friendship, savior, surrogate parent, and love relationships with teachers. These types of relationships, as the case studies in this book document, can lead to emotional pain and heartache and bring more problems into their already complicated lives. Here are examples of how a teacher adviser can spell out the boundaries and limits for a needy student and how administrators and teachers can talk to colleagues who appear to be ignoring the hazards and risks involved in close contact with students

## HOW A TEACHER TALKS TO A STUDENT ABOUT HIS ADVISER ROLE SO BOUNDARIES ARE CLEAR

If a student is looking for a teacher to be a confidant, friend, or surrogate parent who will provide care, nurturing, even love, then teachers need to be able to recognize this process and quickly point out that it is not their role. They need to see it coming and put a stop to it. Divorce, separation, death, or serious illness of a parent can make life appear very treacherous for students. Like all of us, they want a dad, a mom, loving parents, someone to save them from life's blows. When loving parents become absent, teachers are often targeted for that role by needy students. Taking on that role can lead to crossing professional boundaries. Simple words work best for teachers when they try to make clear their helping role and establish professional boundaries. Here is how one teacher approached the issued with a student:

*I am very concerned about your mom and dad's divorce but I can't take over their role. I am your adviser, not your parents. I know you don't like going home after school and would rather spend the time talking to me about your problems. But I have my own family obligations after school. I know there are going to be times when a crisis comes up and you need to talk after school. That's okay once in a while but not on a regular basis. And it's best you don't call me at home. My wife said you called last night. But I do want you to know that I am here to help you. Here is what I can do. I can understand how tough things are and encourage you to keep going. Just what I am doing now. I know you're upset about your dad's leaving and your mom's depression. I know it's tough. But I also know that continuing to feel sorry for yourself doesn't help you move on with your life. Let's do three things that I think will help. First, your grades. Let's talk about how you can get back to work and not let your grades slip any more. Let's be specific and make a plan. Second, let's get your mom in here and talk to her about getting some help. I know a good social service agency that can help her with emergency food and fuel allowances and legal help. Third, I know you are free fourth period. I have an extra help class then with some kids who are going through the same thing as you. I know some of these kids call each other at night and try to help. I know the nights can be rough. Getting involved with them might give you additional support and someone to call at night. Why don't you come by?*

Here our teacher sets the guidelines for his needy student. He shows he wants to help but he can't be a parent. There are definite limits. He indicates that he has his own family responsibilities and calling him at home is not a good thing to do. He suggests an alternative, a fourth period help setting in which other students with similar problems are involved. He keeps his professional boundaries clear. He executes well.

## HOW A VETERAN FEMALE TEACHER WHO IS BECOMING TOO PERSONALLY INVOLVED WITH A STUDENT TALKS ABOUT THE PROBLEM WITH AN ADMINISTRATOR

*I don't get it. I've never been too involved with any of my students. I've always had a line I never crossed. And I've been teaching for twenty years. I thought I'd seen it all. I'm not some naive kid just out of grad school. But I find myself spending more and more time trying to help Frank get through the death of his mother. Actually he's handling the death process pretty well. But I can't seem to let him go on his own. I keep inviting him in for conferences and trying to help. All of a sudden it hit me last week. I'm trying to help too much! I'm the one who needs the contact. I'm the one who likes talking to him and looks forward to our meetings. Here I am, a forty-two-year-old woman acting clueless. I also notice that I've been very lonely since my own divorce. When I meet with Frank it just feels good to talk to someone who needs me. I better do some self-correcting here. Thanks for noticing that I was spending too much time with Frank and inviting me to talk. Sometimes you just don't see things clearly.*

Here the administrator observes a teacher who may be getting too involved with a student. The administrator acts and invites her to talk. The administrator understands that when teachers get involved in too-close relationships with students, it's not just a male phenomenon. Female teachers are also at risk. Another stereotype shot down. Denial out and reality in. Here the administrator provides the teacher with important feedback so she can correct her behavior. If she is left on her own she may cross over her professional boundaries. Therapeutic supervision requires a response to a teacher at risk. It means not looking the other way, hoping the problem will go away or thinking, "It can't happen to her. She has twenty years of experience. She's got to know better." Maybe, right now, she doesn't know better and needs someone to call her attention to it.

## HOW A YOUNG, NAIVE SAVIOR TEACHER GETS NEEDED HELP FROM AN ADMINISTRATOR

Some teachers tend to help with problems that they have personally experienced. For example, if they have experienced an abusive situation as a child or been involved in an abusive situation as an adult, they sometimes become too involved with a student who is experiencing abuse. These teachers know the emotional pain that goes with abuse and they want to help. Effective teacher helpers learn that personal experiences sometimes can lead to overinvolvement with a student whom the teacher may perceive as *going through the same thing as I did.* Professional boundaries must be maintained in spite of the personal experiences and emotional pain of the teacher helper.

Here is how a one-on-one conversation might go between an overinvolved teacher and an administrator:

*It's starting to get to me. All of the kids who have problems with alcoholism in their families keep coming up to my room and talking. At first I thought it was neat. I know how painful it is to have an alcoholic parent. It's something I'll never forget. In fact, that's one of the reasons I went into*

*teaching, to help kids get through these kinds of problems. My tenth grade
English teacher, Mr. Mowbray, helped me through my thing. I wanted to be
just like him. But a lot of these students, particularly the girls, keep suggesting that I am the only one they can trust and that they never had a real
father to talk to about personal things. It's flattering stuff. I even think some
of them have a crush on me. I was dancing with one of those students at the
junior prom last week and I literally had to tear myself away from her. I felt
myself slipping away from my teacher role and getting personally involved.
Let's face it, I'm twenty-five and she's seventeen and a knockout. That's
only a eight-year difference. It's pretty confusing to me as to where my
teacher role ends and a personal relationship begins. I didn't learn anything about this stuff in graduate school. John Proctor, my team teacher,
thinks I've gone too far and I ought to pull back. He suggested that I talk
to you and get some advice. Has this ever happened to you?*

Here the concerned teacher heeds the advice of a fellow teacher who
sees danger ahead. John Proctor's feedback taps into our teacher's own
concerns and questions. Proctor's feedback sends the teacher to the administrator looking for help and a way out of this too-close contact. The
teacher asks good questions of the administrator. Has this ever happened to
you? Where do I draw the line between the role of teacher and personal involvement? The question sets the focus for the one-on-one conversation.
John Proctor throws his colleague a lifeline. His observations and feedback
begin an important learning process for our twenty-five-year-old teacher
that will hopefully lead to an increased awareness and skills to establish
workable professional boundaries. Teachers who care about each other see
trouble coming. There are many teachers like our fictitious John Proctor
who can act to help a colleague avoid sexual harassment, if administrators
signal them that this is an important part of their work as a teacher.

## HOW A COLLEAGUE CONFRONTS A TEACHER
## HEADED TOWARD POSSIBLE SEXUAL MISCONDUCT

Effective teachers don't take a student to lunch alone, invite students to their
home, regularly write notes to a student, or make regular physical contact.
I call these situations *hot spots*. They can get you in trouble. Effective teach-

ers are also more sensitive when they are involved in chaperoning activities such as camping and overnight trips. They know that professional/personal boundaries can sometimes become blurred in these situations.

Here is how a blunt one-on-one conversation goes between a teacher who has experience with how to maintain professional boundaries and an inexperienced teacher who appears to think that helping students can be done only in one-on-one situations away from the school.

*Dave, you are a good teacher. You've got the potential to be the best in the business. But you've got to stop taking kids out to lunch with you one-on-one. You are asking for trouble. I know you want to help the kids and that's a great thing. But don't be naive. When you help, do it in a professional way, in school. I guess I'm trying to be like a big brother to you and suggest there are ways to do things. You can't be every kid's buddy or friend. Like it or not, you are a teacher and you have to act in ways that don't send the wrong message to people. Look at the other teachers in the building who are good helpers and see what they do. Watch Lorraine Jones and Jim Lowry. They meet with kids in the cafeteria or library. I even see them playing hoops in the after-school recreation program. You'd be surprised how much help you can give kids while playing ball with them. And remember this. If I see you going off in your car alone with Gina for lunch one more time, you're going to hear from me. I don't want you fired for appearing to be too involved with students like Gina.*

Here a concerned fellow teacher, one with experience and wisdom, intervenes and confronts the clueless teacher who is not avoiding his hot spots. The teacher becomes the big brother and shows the inexperienced teacher how to proceed safely. He suggests that there is danger, quicksand, ahead; watch out. There are many models and options for help. Take a look at them and learn.

The TSMAI can help motivate teachers to talk about their own search for how to set boundaries and establish a protective barrier they can invoke when the teacher–student relationship becomes too intimate. The inventory helps create conditions where teachers, often for the first time, can voice their concerns about close relationships with students and identify sources of support they can turn to. Here are some examples of teachers' concerns and their search for guidance:

- Learning how to set boundaries usually occurs on the teacher's own watch. In most cases teachers have no training and little supervision on how to proceed. It is a hit-or-miss situation.
- Help often comes from a fellow teacher who voluntarily serves as a big brother or sister and models appropriate behavior in close relationships with students.
- Many teachers are aware that they have favorite students whom they seek out but at the same time are bothered by this behavior. They often feel selfish and think that they are depriving other students of needed attention.
- Many teachers feel a strong emotional tug to help students with difficult personal problems but at the same time think they lack skills in the helping process and sense being drawn into unknown, even dangerous territory. Helping students tends to be a confusing role for teachers who lack training.
- Teachers are also confused when needy students demand more of their attention; many lack skills in how to say "no" or "I can't." The word "frozen" seems to capture their feelings and behavior.
- In terms of sharing thoughts about being attracted to a student, they tend to keep those feelings to themselves or confide in a colleague or friend outside school. They feel it could be harmful to their career and job security to share their thoughts with an administrator.
- They have observed colleagues becoming too involved with students but generally feel it is not their job to intervene.
- Teachers with troubled home lives are often looking for the opportunity to confide in a colleague and share the burden of how these troubles are affecting their teaching performance.

## THE IMPORTANCE OF ONGOING SUPERVISION BY ADMINISTRATORS AND PEER OBSERVATIONS AND SUPPORT IN PREVENTING TEACHER SEXUAL MISCONDUCT

The TSMAI results and the discussions that follow highlight the need for ongoing staff development for teachers in how to be effective in the role of adviser, personal adult advocate, coach, and mentor—all helping roles.

They also point out the important voluntary role that colleagues can play in being a mentor, a big brother or sister, in teaching new teachers how to set boundaries and confronting experienced teachers when they begin to cross boundaries. It's a powerful role for teachers who, through their own hard-won experience, have mastered the tricky ins and outs of helping students while at the same time knowing how to establish clear boundaries. The TSMAI results also suggest the need for administrators to adopt the role of mentor, a big brother or sister, and use their supervision and observation sessions to create a dialogue with teachers on how to handle close contact with students. They must engage teachers in issues other than curriculum, discipline, and so on, and move the supervision conversation into encouraging teachers to disclose information about their home lives, concerns over connecting with certain students, how to help a student with problems, identifying persons they can turn to for help when they have a problem, and so on. In other words they must change the format from a perfunctory session required by the teacher contract into a helping conversation in which the teacher is listened to, guaranteed safety, encouraged to share real concerns, and "taught" by the experienced administrator, now serving as a big brother or big sister instead of a boss, how to deal with the tricky ins and out that come with teaching needy students.

Administrators who become more closely involved with teachers through supervision sessions in which they model how to carry on effective helping relationships are in a real sense teaching staff members how to handle such relationships with students. As I suggest in my book, *An Administrator's Guide to Better Teacher Mentoring*,[11] by modeling how to make contact, establish a trusting relationship, set boundaries for what can be discussed, identify referral resources and sources of support for problems that may need more professional attention and are beyond the expertise of the administrator, how to end a helping conversation, and so on, the administrator takes on the role of a mentor who says "follow my lead." Colleagues such as our fictitious team leader John Proctor, described earlier in this chapter, who is a natural ally and is willing to step up to the plate to help a wayward teacher, can also use this kind of modeling. He doesn't look the other way or say "it's not my job" when it comes to intervention. He sees the problem and acts by confronting the teacher and directing him to an administrator whom he respects and who will offer needed supervision and help. Proctor uses simple helping and confronting words that any responsive citizen would employ upon seeing a neighbor or coworker heading for trouble.

Intervention to help teachers headed toward sexual misconduct is no mystery. It's a two-pronged approach. It requires individual teachers to take notice and have a willingness to confront a colleague. What's important is the contact. It also requires an institutional response, making sure there are many doors in the school are open to both the teacher and vulnerable student. That means expecting administrators and colleagues to observe teacher–student interactions and quickly address any risky behaviors. And it means guidance counselors, social workers, school psychologists, support staff, students, parents, and community members are expected to keep their eyes open on the front lines of the school and share their concern when they see teachers and students involved in risky behavior. They are not expected to be rumormongers or vigilantes but to act as their brothers' keepers and not let members of their school community fall through the cracks and become involved in painful affairs that can ruin the lives of both teacher and students.

## THE NEED FOR TEACHERS TO PASS ON THE SKILLS LEARNED IN SEXUAL MISCONDUCT TRAINING TO STUDENTS

The awareness and skill acquisition obtained through sexual misconduct training should not be limited to administrators and teachers. Learning how to set boundaries is important not only to protect the teacher's professional role but also to teach students how best to navigate through life's problems using many different adult resources. Relying on one teacher or adult figure to meet their needs for friendship, help, and affection can in the end lead to more pain and heartache and serve only to bring more problems into their lives. Administrators do not need a formal training program, a schoolwide conference or an assembly featuring nationally known speakers, or handouts and reading materials that present sexual misconduct as an issue of predator teachers who prey on needy students. These activities, I have suggested, cause teachers, students, and parents to withdraw from supportive contact and miss the important lesson of how students need to learn boundaries and learn to recognize adults they can trust with their problems.

What is needed is to utilize the many open doors of help in the school in which students can join informal, one-on-one, and small group discussions with a focus on how they can find many sources of help from caring adults in the school and community. This process can subtly point out the hazards of relying solely on one savior teacher or adult to guide them through their teen years. As I describe in my books *An Educator's Guide to Understanding the Personal Side of Students' Lives*[12] and *Students in Trouble: Schools Can Help before Failure*,[13] there are many venues in most secondary schools for this learning process to occur. For example, teacher–student adviser conferences; individual and group counseling sessions offered by counselors, social workers, and school psychologists; school nurse–student conversations; training for student peer counseling; conversations between coaches and team members; discipline sessions involving the assistant principal and troubled students; chaperones at school dances and athletic or music events; and the many opportunities for informal conversations between students and caring support staff who are accessible and easy to talk to, such as secretaries in the health, guidance, and administrative offices, hallway and cafeteria monitors, bus drivers, and so on. These many open doors offer all students, from gifted students to potential dropouts, the opportunity to learn from a trusted adult how to find the help they need without risk.

I have found that this kind of process to help students learn about risks in the real world has many parallels in my work in secondary schools as a teacher trainer, school psychologist, student assistance counselor, and guidance counselor. For example, in educating students about the risks of alcohol, drug, and tobacco addiction, I have learned to avoid large conferences and assemblies in which nationally known speakers and reformed addicts address the horrors of addiction. Scare tactics in my view have little impact on students. Instead, I have found that what works to increase student awareness is involving them in a variety of helping conversations offered in the venues described above, conversations in which they explore why they are using substances, what they are getting out of the experience, how they became involved, and, when they are ready, plan how to move out of addictive or potentially addictive behavior. This muted approach can also increase student awareness about setting boundaries and how to avoid risky relationships with savior adults. I believe this approach, like my response to the problem of addiction, has a greater chance for success than alarming students with horror tales of predator teachers.

Our mission is helping students learn which adults they can turn to and which ones to avoid, not simply limiting their education to identifying and avoiding predator adults. We need to provide them with the necessary skills to assess adults in general, those who can be helpful and those who can harm, as they move on from high school into an adult world where they will be called on to form many personal and professional relationships. Simply put, high schools need to offer students learning in who they are, their needs, and which adults can be trusted to help them meet their needs and, in the long run, which adults offer the best opportunity for friendship, caring, love, and support. Alarming and scaring students deprives them of exploring these important questions.

The informal self-awareness conversations I am advocating between caring adults and students in the school need to involve students in looking at their own dark side. That is, how they, like some adults in their lives, ignore the signs of danger ahead in personal relationships and proceed to cross boundaries that lead to pain and hurt, by becoming involved in abusive relationships, developing addictions, hanging with acting-out peers, and even, like Mr. Holland's gifted student Rowena, trying to forge dangerous liaisons with a teacher seen as a friend, savior, surrogate parent, and lover. Here is a helping conversation that might begin with Rowena talking to the school nurse, whom she trusts:

*Things have been so bad at my house. My dad is drinking all the time since he lost his job. My mom is working two jobs now and she is never home. The whole thing scares me. This should be the best time of my life. I am a senior, have the lead role in the musical, and my guidance counselor says maybe I can get a scholarship to college. I am attractive and people like me. They say I have a lot going for me. But all I want is out of my house. I am thinking about going to New York and finding an opportunity in a Broadway show. Mr. Holland says he will help me. He has a close friend in New York with an in with some producers. But—this is so hard to say—I want him to come with me. Silly, isn't it? I am only eighteen and he is married and has a grown son. But I think I love him. I have nobody at home, nobody to love. No, we don't have a loving kind of relationship, and I am sure he doesn't know I feel this way. Maybe you can help me get my head on straight.*

The same kind of interventions need to be offered to the Catherines of the world who fall in love with needy teachers like Joseph Svenden. In *Carried Away* their relationship is "the talk of the town." Everyone in the school and community seems to know, not unlike the cases of Gwendolyn Hampton, Glenn Harris, and Gary Jarvis described in chapter 2. But no one intervenes. Catherine and Joseph are left on their own while their community observes. However, their story might have been different if a school counselor had chosen to break the silence and act. Here is how the counselor might have intervened. The counselor, Sherri North, begins the session.

*Thanks for choosing to meet with me, Catherine. My guess is that my request did not come as a surprise. Over the last month you made a number of appointments to see me but canceled each one. Your mother has done the same thing. I want you to know that I appreciate your showing up today. My sense is that this is very difficult for you but a needed first step. Let me get right to the point. I hope I don't come on too strong but I feel we need to be honest and not waste time. Here is what I see. You seem to be spending every lunch period and after school time with Mr. Svenden. I've also seen you riding around town in his car. And teachers and parents have told me that you've been at his cabin at the lake. It seems to everyone in the school community that you are having some kind of an intimate relationship with him. I am asking you to tell me what's going on and whether you want my help. What are you trying to find in this relationship?*

Catherine is not surprised by Ms. North's comments. She has been wanting to talk to her for months but hesitated each time. Yes, she is very involved with her teacher and yes, she knows their relationship is no secret and is dangerous. Her mother knows and has been nagging her to end the relationship and get some psychological help before she goes to the school and blows the whistle on Svenden. She needs to talk to someone and Ms. North is considered the best counselor in the school and would respect her privacy. Catherine responds:

*Yes, it's all true. I am involved with Joseph. It just kind of happened. I thought I could bring some joy into his life. He seemed so lonely and has all these home troubles. I try to ignore all the stares from the other kids and the teachers but lately it's been difficult. Like there's nowhere to hide in this small town. And I worry that he's going to get into trouble because of my affection and lose his job. That would be just awful because he's a great teacher. The best I've ever had. So dedicated and honest. I blame myself for getting Joseph into all this and I know I should end this thing right now. But every time I make up my mind to tell him it's over, I end up changing my mind. It's like I am frozen and can't speak the words.*

So Ms. North sets the stage for an intervention, counseling Catherine in future sessions on how to make a decision about her relationship and then helping her live with her decision. This intervention will involve counseling Catherine's mother and maybe Joseph Svenden once she gains trust in the counseling relationship. Ms. North is on her own in this intervention. Other members of the school staff seem to view the affair as a soap opera that spices up the discussions in the faculty room. Many students and parents see the affair as flaunting community morals and values and blame Catherine for instigating the relationship. They see her as a bad seed out to ruin the professional and personal life of a decent man. No one seems to see Catherine as a victim except Ms. North. She sees Catherine as a confused teen being swept away into a world in which she has no experience. Finally Catherine has a caring adult in her corner, someone who can guide her.

Like an inexperienced teacher seeking guidance from teammate John Proctor, these are examples of how helpful interventions can be offered to a student. A door is opened by a caring school nurse or counselor for a student to tell his or her story and hopefully find an alternative path. Some readers will probably say these student interventions appear too easy to carry out. However, in my experience I have found that troubled students often respond when they are offered help. Some situations will meet more resistance and tougher words will be needed to wake students up to their dilemma, perhaps words like, "You are asking for trouble. Don't be naive. This relationship is going to add more heartache to your already troubled life. How much of this emotional baggage do you think you can carry around before you collapse? Look at the numbers. You've missed fifteen days this marking period. You're failing three out of five subjects. You've been late to class thirty times and tardy twenty. You've been referred to the child study team. Your mom has been called to try to explain your behavior. According to the school nurse, you've lost twenty-five pounds in two months. A year ago you were on the honor roll and a happy kid. If this relationship with Mr. Svenden is so great, why do you look so unhappy and seem to be literally falling apart? You've got a serious problem that needs to be worked on beginning right now. As the school psychologist I know about kids having troubles and I know how to begin helping them."

However, not every offer to help is met with a positive response by students. The response, "No, I don't have a problem and no, I don't need your help" can also be expected. But such offers serve as a beginning step in intervention. This initial helping conversation unmasks the problem, takes students out of denial, causes them to think seriously about their plight, and shows them where they can turn for help when they are ready.

Teaching students how to learn to set boundaries with peers, romantic relations, parents, teachers, coaches, and significant adults in their lives can also be done in small groups facilitated by counselors, social workers, and school psychologists, as well as being part of training students to be peer counselors. Boundary setting can also be taught as part of the curriculum in health and English classes. For example, in health class students learn positive behaviors and how to seek out reliable adult role models. In English they learn from literature how teens and adults face their own dark sides and avoid being lured into damaging relationships.

In fact, teaching students about boundaries and how to form healthy relationships is finally becoming a part of the national discussion on how to prepare students for the personal aspects of teen and adult life. Over the past thirty years academics have been developing the study of "close relationships," forming the International Association for Relationship Research to share resources and data.[14] Such research is "not just about what makes people happy but how relationships can affect other things, for example, someone's health," says Lisa Baker, assistant professor of psychology at Purchase College, part of the State University of New York. According to Irvine, in recent years some professors have moved beyond theory, making the discussion more personal by teaching relationship skills they can use outside the classroom. Lecture topics and workshops offered at an increasing number of colleges and universities include Falling in Love without Losing Your Mind and How to Break Up without Falling Apart. The latter class includes discussions on how to end a relationship cleanly. As Irvine reports, some academics question whether classes like these belong in college setting, but others say there is no reason love should be ignored.

I argue that teenagers should be offered the same kind of learning opportunities on how to form healthy relationships and end those that bring harm, abuse, and isolation. Having students learn about relationships in secondary school can help them avoid potential pitfalls as they navigate through the many problems of teen life. They shouldn't have to wait until college for such training or, for students going directly into the workplace, receive no training at all. Yet secondary schools are increasingly busy places with many mandates. Arguing to set up additional courses in relationship building would draw instant resistance from administrators and teachers already hard-pressed for resources and time. But I suggest that relationship-building skills that include learning to set boundaries, form healthy relationships, and end destructive ones can be easily added on to the many existing helping and curriculum venues I described above and serve to help the Rowenas and Catherines in our schools avoid the hazards and risks that ill-advised love relationships can bring. Waiting to offer students such training can create a climate for sexual misconduct, with smitten students involved with needy teachers and lacking the skills and know-how to avoid or end such relationships, frozen and not knowing how to say no.

In conclusion, teacher sexual misconduct is more apt to happen when teachers and students lack this kind of supervision, peer support, and commitment by the entire school community to act as their brothers' keepers. I am advocating that effective teachers need an ongoing support network to which they can turn for help with professional and personal problems. Each secondary school needs clear, well-lit, open doors for help, the kinds of help available for a myriad of problems, not simply those related to academic teaching. No professional life is without trouble or trying times. Good teaching years can be followed by a year or years filled with failure. What works one year for students fails the next year. While teaching careers are sometimes described as one steady experience, the reality is that there are many ups and downs. Teachers' obituaries tend to be the same: "John Franklin taught history at Worcester North High School for thirty-three years." But for most teachers, each year in their teaching career is different. The best of us can come across situations in which we begin to doubt our competency and skill. And no area is more difficult to exit than becoming too personally involved with a student. It puts teachers in a double bind. They desperately need to talk about the problem but they are afraid, sometimes justifiably, that if they ask for help they will be labeled as a teacher who is over the line, out of control, often for the rest of their career. It is not easy for students or teachers to move beyond a negative label. Caring administrators and colleagues like John Proctor can offer these troubled teachers the beginning help they need, not, as is often the practice, leave them be, alone, isolated, and labeled as a bad apple that the administration and community would like to see vanish. The caring, sometimes blunt feedback from the John Proctors of the world starts the healing process and offers the opportunity to plan how to separate oneself from over-involvement.

An important component of training, therefore, is to have teachers identify people in their support network who will help if needed and not turn them away. If they can't list anyone, which is not unusual, then training needs to help them learn how to enlist such support. The training also needs to ask teachers to identify the colleagues they help on a regular basis. This process helps remind teachers that they need to serve as their brother's keeper and not let one colleague fall through the cracks. We do have a responsibility to guard the welfare of colleagues as well as students and parents.

In the end, my message is that each of us as educators can at some point in our careers become at risk. We need caring, skilled administrators and colleagues in our corner to help us find our way. And we need to pass on our training in sexual misconduct so students also learn how to set boundaries, form healthy relationships, and end destructive ones. They too need to be prepared for the complexities that come with close relationships.

## NOTES

1. Elaine Yaffe, "Expensive, Illegal, and Wrong: Sexual Harassment in Our Schools," *Phi Delta Kappa* (Special Report November 1995), 37.
2. Caroline Hendrie, "Cost Is High When Schools Ignore Abuse," *Education Week*, 9 December 1998, http://www.edweek.org/ew/vol-18/15handle.h18 (accessed 13 August 2004).
3. Michael Levinson, "Ex-principal Rejects Naming Honor," boston.com, 12 December 2004, http://boston.com/news/local/articles/2004/12/ex_principal_rejects_naming_hon (accessed 12 December 2004).

4. Anthony W. Jackson and Gayle A. Davis, *Turning Points 2000: Educating Adolescents in the 21st Century* (New York: Teachers College Press, 2000), 140–44.

5. National Association of Secondary School Principals (NASSP), *Executive Summary of Breaking Ranks II: Strategies for Leading High School Reform* (Reston, VA: National Association of Secondary School Principals, 2004), 1–6.

6. Caroline Hendrie, "Sexual Abuse by Educators Is Scrutinized," *Education Week*, 10 March 2004, http://www.edweek.org/ew/ewstory.cfmlug=26Abuse.h23 (accessed 18 March 2004).

7. Caroline Hendrie, "Preventing Sexual Misconduct," *Education Week*, 10 March 2004, http://www.edweek.org/ew/ewstory.cfm?slug=26Abuse-B1.h23& keywords=sexual%20ab (accessed 9 September 2004).

8. Caroline Hendrie, "Report Examining Sexual Misconduct Taps Some Nerves," *Education Week*, 14 July 2004, http://www.edweek.org/ew/ew_print story.cfm?slug=42Abuse.h23 (accessed 22 July 2004).

9. ChucksConnection Film Review, "Mr. Holland's Opus," http://www.chucks connection.com/holland.html (accessed 2 September 2004).

10. Fine Line Features Synopsis, "Carried Away," http://finelinefeatures.com/ carried/synopsis.htm (accessed 2 September 2004).

11. William L. Fibkins, *An Administrator's Guide to Better Teacher Mentoring* (Lanham, MD: Scarecrow Press, 2002), 173.

12. William L. Fibkins, *An Educator's Guide to Understanding the Personal Side of Their Students' Lives* (Lanham, MD: Scarecrow Press, 2004), 245.

13. William L. Fibkins, *Students in Trouble: Schools Can Help before Failure* (Lanham, MD: Scarecrow Press, 2005), 91–161.

14. Martha Irvine, "Colleges Offer Classes on Relationships," Yahoo!News .com, 13 February 2005, http://yahoo.com/news?tmpl=story&cid=514&u=ap/ 20050213/ap_on_re_us/teaching (accessed 14 February 2005).

# References

Archibold, Randall C., "A Chill at Stuyvesant High," *New York Times*, 21 September 1999, 1, 8 (B).

Associated Press, "Evidence Against Teacher Barred," boston.com, 13 October 1994, http://nl.newsbank.com/nl-search/we/Archives?p_action=print (accessed 20 November 2004).

——, "Maine Teen-ager Testifies of Sex with Ex-teacher," *Boston Globe*, 9 March 1995, 26.

——, "Maine Third-Grade Teacher Acquitted of Sexually Abusing Two Teen-Age Boys," *Boston Globe*, 11 March 1995, 14 (Metro).

Boyle, Maureen, "Detective Lyons Investigated Shockro Case 'Relentlessly,'" SouthCoastToday.com, 8 January 1998, http://www.s-t.com/daily/01-98/01-98/a01o003.htm (accessed 9 November 2004).

Boyle, Maureen, and Bridgette Sweeney, "From Trust to Betrayal and Lingering Pain," SouthCoastToday.com, 31 December 1997, http://southcoasttoday.com/daily/12-97/12-31-97/a01lo005.htm (accessed 8 November 2004).

Briggs, Bill, "Coach's Harsh Style Brings Success, But Some Wonder If It's Worth It," DenverPost.com, 12 October 2003, http://www.denverpost.com/cda/print/?.1674.36%7E76%7E1690925.html (accessed 2 January 2005).

——, "Lopez: Hoopsters Not about Money," DenverPost.com, 12 October 2003, http://www.denverpost.com/Stories/0.1413,36%7E76%7E1692617.00.html (accessed 2 January 2005).

——, "Success a Constant among Lopez's Teams," DenverPost.com, 12 October 2003, http://www.denverpost.com/cda/article/print/0.1674.36%7E76%7E169074.00.html (accessed 2 January 2005).

Buettner, Russ, "Teacher, Teen on the Run for Love," *Newsday*, 11 May 1995, 6 (A).

Carnegie Council on Adolescent Development: Task Force on Education of Young Adolescents, *Turning Points: Preparing American Youth for the 21st Century*, Washington, DC: Carnegie Council on Adolescent Development, 1989.

145

ChucksConnection Film Review, "Mr. Holland's Opus," http://www.chuckscon-nection.com/holland.html (accessed 2 September 2004).

Colorado Hoopsters, *News & Announcements*, January–February 2005, http://coloradohoopsters.com (accessed 2 January 2005).

Demoretcky, Tom, "Teacher Cleared of Fondling," *Newsday*, 26 January 2000, 29 (A).

DenverChannel.com, "Girls' Basketball Coach May Face 100 Counts Related to Sexual Assaults," 20 August 2004, http://www.thedenverchannel.com/print/ 3669544/detail/html (accessed 2 January 2005).

*Education Week*, "Preventing Sexual Misconduct," March 10, 2004, http://www.edweek.org/ew/ewstory.cfm?slug=26B1,h23&keywords=sex-ual%2ab (accessed 18 September 2004).

Estrella, John, "10 days of Allegations, Questions, and Headlines," SouthCoast-Today.com, 23 February 1997, http://www.southcoasttoday.com/daily/02-97/02-23-97/a011o005.htm (accessed 8 November 2004).

Farkas, Steve, and Jean Johnson, "Kids These Days: What Americans Really Think about the Next Generation," *Public Agenda* (1999): 8–9, 11, 13, 16–19, 25–26.

Feller, Ben, "Sexual Misconduct in Schools Tabulated," Associated Press, 1 July 2004, http://info.mgnetwork.com/printhispage.cgi?url=http%3A//www.tampa-trib.com?news?M (accessed 14 August 2004).

Fibkins, William L., *An Administrator's Guide to Better Teacher Mentoring*, Lanham, MD: Scarecrow Press, 2002.

———, *An Educator's Guide to Understanding the Personal Side of Their Students' Lives*, Lanham, MD: Scarecrow Press, 2003.

———, *Preventing Teacher Sexual Misconduct*, Bloomington, IN: Phi Delta Kappa Foundation, 1996.

———, *Students in Trouble: Schools Can Help before Failure*, Lanham, MD: Scarecrow Press, 2005.

Fillo, Mary Ellen, "Shadows Stalked Girls' Glory Days," Associated Press, 10 March 2002, 5–7 (A1).

Fine Line Features Synopsis, *Carried Away,* http://www.finelinefeatures.com/ carried/synopsis.htm (accessed 2 September 2004).

Finn, Robin, "Growth in Women's Sports Stirs Harassment Issues," *New York Times*, 7 March 1999, 1 (A), 24 (L).

Gabbard, G. O., J. D. Bloom, C. C. Nadelson, and M. T. Norman, eds., *Psychodynamic Approaches to Physicians' Sexual Misconduct*, Washington D.C.: American Psychiatric Press, 1991.

Goldberg, Carey, "Manhattan Teacher Surrenders in Kidnapping of Teen-age Girl," *New York Times*, 17 May 1995, 1 (A), 4 (B).

——, "Nationwide Hunt for Teacher and Girl, 15," *New York Times*, 11 May 1995, 1, 8 (B).

*Hartford Courant* editorial, "End Mr. McKernan's Career," *Hartford Courant*, 4 June 2004, 10 (A).

Hendrie, Caroline, "Abuse by Women Raises Its Own Set of Problems," *Education Week*, 2 December 1998, http://www.edweek.org/ew/vol-18/14women .h18 (accessed 13 August 2004).

——, "Cost Is High When Schools Ignore Abuse, " *Education Week*, 9 December 1998, http://www.edweek.org/ew/vol-18/15handle.h18 (accessed 13 August 2004).

——, "Experts Convene on Sexual Abuse by Teachers," *Education Week*, 9 April 2003, http://www.edweek.org/ew/ewstory.cfm?slug=30abuse.h22 (accessed 8 August 2004).

——, "In Youth's Tender Emotions Abusers Find Easy Pickings," *Education Week*, 2 December 1998, http://www.edweek.org/ew/vol-18/14tactic.h18 (accessed 13 August 2004).

——, "Preventing Sexual Misconduct," *Education Week*, 10 March 2004, http://www.edweek.org/ewstory.cfm?slug=26Abuse-B1.h23&keywords= sexual%20ab (accessed 9 September 2004).

——, "Report Examining Sexual Misconduct Taps Some Nerves," *Education Week*, 14 July, 2004, http://www.edweeek.org/ew/ew_printstory.cfm.?slug+42 Abuse.h23 (accessed 22 July 2004).

——, "Sex with Students: When Employees Cross the Line," *Education Week*, 2 December 1998, http://www.edweek.org/ew/vol-18/14abuse.18 (accessed 13 August 2004).

——, "Sexual Abuse by Educators Is Scrutinized, " *Education Week*, 10 March 2004, http://www.edweek.org/ew/ewstory.cfm?slug=26Abuse.h23 (accessed 18 March 2004).

Herbert, Bob, "An Ugly School Situation," *New York Times*, 17 May 1995, 19 (A).

Irvine, Martha, "Colleges Offer Classes on Relationships," Yahoo!News.com, 13 February 2005, http://www.yahoo.com/news?tmpl=story&cid=514&u=ap/ 20050213/ap_On_re_us/teaching (accessed 14 February 2005).

Jackson, Anthony W., and Gayle A. Davis, *Turning Points 2000: Educating Adolescents in the 21st Century*, New York: Teachers College Press, 2000.

Jacobs, Andrew, "School Official Charged with Molesting Students, " *New York Times*, 22 May 1999, 3 (B).

Kane, Arthur, Adam Thompson, and Bill Briggs, "Coach in Sex Case Apparent Suicide," DenverPost.com, 12 December 2004, http://www.denverpost.com/cda/ article/print/0.1674.36%7E53%7E262282.00.html (accessed 2 January 2005).

Kaufman, Susan, "When Teachers Mix Socially with Students," *News & Observer*, 29 September 1994, 1, 12 (A).

Kreytak, Steven, "Gym Teacher Charged with Rape," *Newsday*, 8 March 2000, 8 (A).

Kreytak, Steven, and Gregg Sarra, "'Connection' Broken," *Newsday*, 11 November 1999, 5, 60 (A).

Lam, Chau, "No Jail for Coach in Affair," *Newsday*, 21 March 2000, 29 (A).

Levinson, Michael, "Ex-principal Rejects Naming Honor," boston.com, 12 December 2004, http://boston.com/news/local/articles/2004/12/ex_principal_rejects_naming_hon (accessed 12 December 2004).

Mattson, Rick, "Mr. Holland's Opus," http://ransomfellowship.org/M_MrHolland.html (accessed 2 September 2004).

Mohan, Geoffrey, "Guilty in Teen Sex," *Newsday*, 22 February 1997, 27 (A).

Moy, Kimberly W., and William Schubert, "Coaches Avoid Charges in Sex Allegations," *Hartford Courant*, 10 January 2002, 7 (A1).

Murphy, Shelley, "Teacher in Abuse Suit Defends Actions," boston.com, 14 September 2004, http://www.boston.com/news/local/articles/2004/09/14/teacher_in_abuse_suit_defends_act (accessed 15 December 2004).

National Association of Secondary School Principals (NASSP), *Breaking Ranks: Changing an American Institution*, Reston, VA: National Association of Secondary Principals, 1996, 1–29.

——, *Executive Summary of Breaking Ranks II: Strategies for Leading High School Reform*, Reston, VA: National Association of Secondary School Principals, 2004, 1–6.

Noguera, Pedro, "Special Topics: Transforming High Schools, " *Education Leadership*, May 2004, http://www.ascd.org/publications/ed_lead/200405/noguera.html (accessed 4 June 2004).

O'Brien, Ellen, "Police Press Questions to School in Rape Case," *Boston Sunday Globe*, 16 February 1997, 4 (B).

O'Hagan, Maureen, and Christine Willmsen, "Misconduct Often Goes Unpunished by Districts," SeattleTimes.com, 15 December 2003, http://seattletimes.nwsource.com/news/local/coaches/news/daytwo.html (accessed 11 January 2005).

——, "What School Districts Can Do," SeattleTimes.com, 15 December 2003, http://seattletimes.nwsource.com/news/local/coaches/news/school.html (accessed 11 January 2005).

Ontario Province Ministry of the Attorney General, "Chapter I: The Nature and Scope of the Review," Review of Kenneth DeLuca Case, 1999, http://attorney general.jus.gov.on.ca/english/about/pubs/robins/ch1.asp (accessed 26 February 2005).

———, "Chapter III: Extent and Nature of Teacher–Student Sexual Misconduct," Review of Kenneth DeLuca Case, 1999, http://attorneygeneral.jus .gov.on.ca/english/about/pubs/robins/ch.3.asp (accessed 26 February 2005).

Quintanilla, Blanca Monica, "Track Coach Faces Molestation Charges," *Newsday*, 22 July 1998, 29 (A).

Rhode, David, "Probation for Teacher Guilty of Abuse at Stuyvesant," *New York Times*, 19 August 1999, 1 (B).

Salcedo, Michele, "Teacher in Rape Case Popular in School," *Newsday*, 22 February 1995, 7 (A).

Sheehan, Peter, "Safety for All Is Goal of Background Screening, Training," *Long Island Catholic*, 20 October 2004, 1, 3.

Simmons, Roberta G., and Dale A. Blyth, *Moving Into Adolescence: The Impact of Puberty Changes and School Context*, New York: Aldine De Gruyter, 1987.

Slade, Margot, "Yes, Statutory Rape Is Still a Rather Big Deal," *New York Times*, 11 June 1995, 9 (E).

Smith, Estelle Lander, "Jail for Teacher in Student's Sex Abuse," *Newsday*, 19 July 1994, 4 (A).

———, "Teen to Testify at Teacher Sex Trial," *Newsday*, 6 May 1994, 25 (A).

Sorrentino, Mary Ann, "John Shockro Not the Only Guilty Party in Sordid Case," SouthCoastToday.com, 7 January 1998, http://www.s-t.com/daily/01-07-98/c04op105.htm (accessed 8 November 2004).

*Southington Journal*, "Town's Disgust Outlasts a Statute of Limitations," *New York Times*, 14 January 2002, 17 (A).

Stover, Del, "What Happens When a Teacher Accused of Harassment Is Innocent?" National School Boards Association, 16 May 2000, http://www.nsba .org/site/print.asp?TRACKID=&VID=58&ACTION=PRINT&CID=332& (accessed 9 September 2004).

Swiggart, William, Karen Starr, Reid Finlayson, and Anderson Spickard, "Sexual Boundaries and Physicians: Overview and Educational Approach to the Problem," Vanderbilt University Center for Professional Health, 2001, http://www.mc.vanderbilt.edu/root/vumc.php?site=cph&doc=742 (accessed 13 August 2004).

Theisen, Sylvester P., "Interfaith Sexual Trauma Institute (ISTI) Book Review of John C. Gonsiorek (ed.), *Breach of Trust, Sexual Exploration by Health Career Professionals and Clergy*," 22 April 1996, http://www.csbsju.edu/isti/ Book%20Reviews/gonsiorek.html (accessed 13 August 2004).

Thompson, Adam, "Summer Tourneys Where It's At for College Hopefuls," DenverPost.com, 12 October 2003, http://www.denverpost.com/Stories/0.1413.36%7E76%1690740.00.html (accessed 2 January 2005).

Thompson, Adam, and Bill Briggs, "Cult of Personality," DenverPost.com, 12 October 2003, http://www.denverpost.com/cda/article/print.0.1674.36% 7E76%7E1692763.00.html (accessed 2 January 2005).

———, "Sex Charges Shadow Girls' Coach," DenverPost.com, 12 October 2003, http://www.denverpost.com/cda/article/print/0.1674.36%7E76%7E1693470.0 0.html (accessed 2 January 2005).

Tieffer, Leonore, "On the Therapist's Couch, " *Newsday*, 5 January 1997, 37 C.

Vaishnav, Anand, "Top Official Targets Abuse by Educators: Driscoll to Urge Vigilance," boston.com, 24 August 2004, http://www.boston.com/news/ local/articles/2004/08/24/top_official_targets_abuse_by_ed (accessed 25 August 2004).

Willmsen, Christine, and Maureen O'Hagan, "Coaches Continue Working for Schools and Private Teams after Being Caught for Sexual Misconduct," SeattleTimes.com, 14 December 2000, http://seattletimes.nwsource.com/news/local/coaches/news/dayone.html (accessed 11 January 2005).

———, "Misconduct Registry, More Training Needed for Washington Coaches," SeattleTimes.com, 16 December 2003, http://seattletimes.nwsource.com.news .local/coaches/news/state.html (accessed 11 January 2005).

Wishnietsky, Dan, "Reported and Underreported Teacher–Student Sexual Harassment," *Journal of Education Research*, *3* (1991): 164–69.

Wyatt, Edward, "Schools Show Jump in Reports of Sex Abuse," *New York Times*, 23 May 2001, 1, 7 (B).

Yaffe, Elaine, "Expensive, Illegal, and Wrong: Sexual Harassment in Our Schools," *Phi Delta Kappa* (special report, November 1995): 37.

Yan, Ellen, and Robin Topping, "School Sex Abuse: Sachem H.S. Teacher Held in Case Involving Teen, " *Newsday*, 25 June 1993, 3 (A).

Zehr, Mary Ann, "Report Tallies Alleged Sexual Abuse by Priests," *Education Week*, 10 March 2004, http://www.edweek.org/ew/ew_printstory.cfm?slug=26 Catholic.h23 (accessed 13 August 2004).

# About the Author

**William L. Fibkins** is a writer, university professor, education consultant, and lecturer specializing in training school administrators, teacher leaders, and school counselors on how to develop school-based teacher training centers and student support services. His training programs also include leadership and peer counseling training for student leaders; drug, alcohol, and tobacco intervention for students on the road to addiction; and training parents as reliable sources of help and referral for students and parents headed toward the margins of school life.

Fibkins holds degrees in education, counselor education, and school administration from Syracuse University and the University of Massachusetts. Fibkins's publications include *The Empowering School: Getting Everyone on Board to Help Teenagers* (1995), *The Teacher-As-Helper Training Manual* (1998), *What Schools Should Do to Help Kids Stop Smoking* (2000), *An Administrator's Guide to Better Teacher Mentoring* (2002), *An Educator's Guide to Understanding the Personal Side of Students' Lives* (2003), and *Students in Trouble: Schools Can Help before Failure* (2005). He is also the author of numerous professional monographs on restructuring secondary schools, training teachers as advisers, restructuring secondary school guidance services, designing and implementing group counseling programs, and developing school-based health centers to address teen health issues.

Fibkins's in-school experience includes serving as founder and director of the Stony Brook University–Bay Shore Public Schools Teacher Training Center, director of teacher training for the Queens College–Louis Armstrong Intermediate School, and founder of the student assistance counseling program at the Shoreham-Wading River, New York, school district as well as chair of the Curriculum Development Committee at Shoreham. His university experience includes teaching in the school administration program at Queens College, New York City, and the Counseling and Human Development program at Long Island University, C.W. Post Campus, Brookville, New York.